WHY
THE F*CK
CAN'T I
CHANGE?

WHY THE F*CK CAN'T I CHANGE?

DR GABIJA TOLEIKYTE

Thread

Published by Thread in 2021

An imprint of Storyfire Ltd.
Carmelite House
50 Victoria Embankment
London EC4Y 0DZ

www.thread-books.com

ISBN: 978-1-80019-272-0
eBook ISBN: 978-1-83888-992-0

The information contained in this book is not advice and the
method may not be suitable for everyone to follow. This book is not
intended to replace the services of trained professionals or to be a
substitute for medical advice. You are advised to consult a doctor on
any matters relating to your health, and in particular on any matters
that may require diagnosis or medical attention.

To my family

CONTENTS

INTRODUCTION

Have you ever come up with amazing New Year's resolutions like losing weight, starting to save money, setting up your own business, exercising regularly, changing your career, eating more healthily or quitting smoking? You probably pumped yourself up full of enthusiasm and the belief that this year will be very different.

Fast-forward, and what happened a month down the line? If you are like the majority of us, you probably went back to where you started. This is something I see in most of my coaching clients and the attendees of my seminars, my friends and, to be honest, in my own life. We all do it.

In my coaching practice, I have seen people struggling to change harmful habits for years and even decades. When I first began coaching, I was mainly working with university professors, department heads and lecturers. And, guess what, they faced the same problems too. Some struggled to stop procrastinating and were always leaving things to the last minute and missing important deadlines. Others could not force themselves to eat more healthily or exercise, even experiencing serious health issues. Other clients attended workshop after workshop on empowering leadership and still, while under stress, struggled to incorporate all the useful insights they had learned in practice.

The process of trying and failing to change is totally soul-destroying – we have learned to believe that if only we try hard enough and have the willpower, we should be able to change. When we fail to change, we start to doubt our own abilities and personalities, and we develop low self-esteem. The unrealistic expectations we have for our brains are not only bad for our own relationship with ourselves, but also, by causing additional stress, make it even harder for us to create real, lasting change. Thus, learning what we can realistically expect from our brains and having practical ways to create change can break this vicious cycle.

Our brains resist sudden change for multiple reasons. Humans are creatures of habit, because following habits automatically requires a lot less energy and mental space, freeing us up to focus on other things. Also, familiarity comforts the emotional centres of our brains. We form habits subconsciously without even realising it and often struggle to change them. Each time we try and fail to implement a change, we accumulate disappointment and start to lose hope. Everybody does it.

In order to stop repeating past mistakes, we need to understand why we formed these habits in the first place, and what we got out of it. Our actions always feed important needs, such as safety, variety, significance, connection. If we didn't get anything from our actions, we wouldn't do them anymore. That's why we cannot simply get rid of old habits; we need first to understand the purpose they serve. Only then can we work out how to get the same rewards in a better way. That's where this book comes in.

To implement lasting change, we need to manage conflict between different centres of the brain. We can group the areas of the brain into three major classes, based on our evolutionary development: the lizard brain, the mammal brain and the human brain. These three brain classes are in fact groupings of multiple areas of the brain, but for the sake of simplicity, I'll just refer to 'lizard', 'mammal' and 'human' brains.

The lizard brain controls automatic functions such as breathing, heartbeat and digestion, and is essentially in place before we are born. The mammal brain automatises our actions – creating habits, physical skills and remembering past events – to ensure we can survive in our environment. The mammal brain's main objective is to keep us safe, and communicates 'safe/not safe' to our other centres by creating emotions. The human brain is the smartest and the most up-to-date part, and enables us to make sense of the world, learn, and have individual personality traits, language, abstract thoughts and empathy for others.

Together, these brain centres enable us to make sound decisions, resist temptation, control our temper and understand other people. But this divide of functions within the brain can sometimes create problems. The mammal brain always seeks safety and pleasure, whereas the human brain wants to make the best choices, to learn, develop and create change, to keep growing and optimising our lives. This can often lead to inner conflict.

In situations of uncertainty or threat, the mammal brain creates the emotions we hate such as anger, jealousy, fear and anxiety. The mammal brain's aim here is to push us to avoid uncertain or threatening situations. As if stirring up negative emotions wasn't powerful enough, the mammal brain can temporarily 'switch off' the rational centres of the brain, making us incapable of rationally assessing the situation and often causing behaviour we later regret. In other words, the human brain, which we might see as the responsible adult in the room, gets shut down.

In order to make the best decisions, have the most fulfilling relationships and create lasting change in our lives, we need to provide our brains with three things: enough energy for the human brain, especially the smartest centre of it called the prefrontal cortex (PFC for short), safety for the mammal brain and enough repetition to create strong neural networks we call 'brain highways'.

Moreover, to change our behaviour in areas such as decision-making, communication and relationship dynamics, we also need to know what conditions are needed for our brains to function optimally.

I have divided this book into nine chapters, covering the neurological basis of each aspect of the 'self' and what is needed for us to create behavioural change in each area.

The first three chapters cover the first part of the book: Changing the Self. In Chapter One, Changing Your Habits, I look at why we develop habits and why we struggle so much to change them. I also cover why we have bad habits in the first place and how we can replace them with better alternatives. If you feel lukewarm about creating change, this chapter will also help you to increase your motivation and long-term vision for where you truly want to go.

In Chapter Two, Changing Your Emotions, I discuss why we feel the way we do, what our emotions are telling us and how we can change them. Emotions are mainly created by the mammal brain and controlled or suppressed by the PFC, the smartest part of the human brain. The emotional component of our existence is the hardest to change, since it is created by the subconscious centres of our brains. To change our emotions, we need to understand why we have them in the first place, what they are 'telling' us and how our actions can influence them.

In Chapter Three, Changing Your Personality, I first cover the neurological basis of forming our identity: how we perceive the world, how we remember it and how we use that data to build our own internal model of the world. Each stage of this process is full of biases, and each of us forms a very different worldview. Needless to say, these views influence our personality traits and the decisions we make. So, if we want to create a real shift in this area, we need to accept the flaws in our model of the world and challenge them. At the end of Chapter Three, I discuss the characteristics of fixed and growth mindsets, based on the work of Carol Dweck (2017), and how these influence our ability to change.

The second part of the book, Changing the Results, is dedicated to creating better outcomes in our lives.

In Chapter Four, Changing Your Productivity, I discuss the neuroscience behind the key qualities of getting things done: memory, attention, prioritising and willpower, and how we can gradually strengthen them. And, of course, I cover why we procrastinate and I suggest some practical tools for reducing procrastination. This topic is highly popular in my public talks.

In Chapter Five, Changing Your Brain Health, I cover the conditions our brains need in order to feel sharp, be in a good mood and have the ability to change. I will take you through the chemical basis of brain activity (brain chemicals called neurotransmitters) and how our day-to-day actions – food, drink, exercise, sleep, meditation and so on – influence them.

In Chapter Six, Changing Your Decision-Making, I cover the neurological basis of rational and emotional decisions. This chapter helps you to understand rational and emotional decision-making, the problems with each system and ways to combine them to make better decisions in the future. It starts by discussing the System I (emotional, fast) and System II (rational, slow) models of Daniel Kahneman, author of *Thinking, Fast and Slow* (2011). I later move on to the experiments of neuroscientists such as Antonio Damasio (author of *Descartes' Error* (2006)) to look at exact brain regions involved in rational and emotional processing and challenge the idea that they are completely separate systems. I also cover why we sometimes get stuck in the decision-making process, often called 'analysis paralysis', and offer practical tools on how to get unstuck.

The third part of the book, Changing Relationships, consists of three more chapters crucial for understanding and changing the dynamics of personal and professional relationships.

In Chapter Seven, Changing Your Leadership, I share the insights I've developed from another very popular seminar, looking at leadership in both the personal and the professional sense. I cover different styles of leadership: task-focused dissonant leadership and relationship-focused resonant leadership. I look at what happens in our brains when we engage in each of these styles of leadership, what happens in the brains of others with whom we interact, and which style is more beneficial. Last but not least, I share what happens in our brains when we are stressed and how stress affects our leadership styles. This is followed by practical tips on how to reduce stress in ourselves and the people around us.

In Chapter Eight, Changing Your Relationships, I discuss how early childhood affects the dynamics of our relationships in the future and look at practical tools for dealing with this. Mammal brain areas need lots of safety and they 'freak out' if we trigger past traumas. Healing these traumas requires environments and relationships that provide enough safety and predictability for the mammal brain to override old scripts. Of course, that relies on choosing people who are suitable for us in the first place, so I cover the romantic phase of love and why we are often attracted to people who cause us pain. Then we move on to the second stage of relationships – the power struggle – and the practical steps that can help us to move on to the lasting love and true partnership stage of the relationship.

Finally, in Chapter Nine, Changing Your Communication, I discuss mammal-brain- and human-brain-dominant thinking and the types of conversations we are capable of when trapped in each mode. In brief, mammal-brain-dominant thinking, which we get trapped in when we are exhausted or emotionally challenged, can only produce attack or withdrawal from the conversation. However, when rested and in a good state emotionally, we are able to engage in human-brain-dominant thinking which is capable of much more constructive kinds of conversations: debate (when we share points of view and knowledge) and dialogue (when, in addition to the information, we also share our feelings). I also cover what thinking and communication skills these different types of conversations evoke in other people, and there are practical tips on what to do if you catch yourself or the other person in the mammal-brain-dominant communication mode.

The book ends with the Conclusion where, using the example of my client Emily, I demonstrate how these nine topics fit together. As a result, you should be able to understand your own behaviour, and why you have previously got stuck, and you will have practical tools for creating change. My dream is that this book becomes your companion in getting to know your true self by learning about the inner mechanisms of your brain. Using the practical tools, you should be able to create lasting change that is congruent with what your brain needs – honouring your character, your values and your history. I hope that in reading this you will have fun and feel less alone in the sometimes frustrating journey of self-change.

PART I

Changing the Self

CHAPTER ONE

Changing Your Habits

In this chapter, you will learn:

- How and why we create habits.
- Why it is difficult for us to get rid of bad habits.
- How you can get motivated to change unwanted habits in any area of your life.
- Whether it is better to go cold turkey or to change things slowly.
- What the brain needs to make change last.

Andrew wakes up early in the morning. As soon as he opens his eyes his mind starts to buzz with so many thoughts that his stress levels begin to rise, even before he has had time to make his first cup of coffee. He nervously jumps in the shower and starts getting ready for work. By the time he is dressed, his appetite is wrecked by an overwhelming sense of anxiety and he leaves home without eating breakfast. Andrew jumps on the train and by the time the train reaches its destination his stomach is rumbling like a drum, so he grabs a large milky coffee and a blueberry muffin in the coffee shop and consumes them quickly, pacing through the station.

This is just a short snapshot of Andrew's Monday. However, if we were to track Andrew throughout the week, we would realise that his daily habits are quite consistent. In fact, Andrew has been struggling to change them for a few years. He came to me trying to change his work-life balance as his daily habits were pushing him into anxiety attacks, weight gain, high blood pressure, type II diabetes, an impaired relationship with his family and poor performance at work.

You might currently be judging Andrew, or secretly thinking that you are not that different from him. Either way, we are all the same – most of the time we form habits effortlessly and unconsciously and become aware of them only when we start to face their negative consequences over time, or when we try to change them.

In fact, our brains were designed to create and maintain habits to save energy and ensure quick reaction times. To change our habits, we need to create new networks in the brain, ones that encode new habits and also weaken the existing networks that are producing these undesirable habits. This process requires not only time, but lots of energy, consistency and action of the right magnitude. It seems like a clear process, but it's a difficult one to stick to in practice as the mammal brain often tries to bring us back to our old ways. In this chapter, I describe in detail what happens in each stage of this process and what obstacles there are, and I share practical tips on how to move forward if you get stuck in any of these stages.

One brain, three parts

Our brains didn't develop in a day. It has taken millions of years for the human brain to reach its current state, with different parts evolving at different times.

According to the Triune Brain model, developed by Paul MacLean (1990), the most ancient centres of our brains are grouped into the so-called paleo-reptilian complex (or the lizard brain for short). The lizard brain controls our vital functions, such as breathing, digestion and heartbeat, and similar centres can be found in the brains of current reptiles, hence the name.

On top of the lizard brain we find another cluster of more recent centres, responsible for keeping us safe, called the paleo-mammalian complex (or the mammal brain for short). The mammal brain enables us to acquire skills and habits, creating automatic routines to ensure quick reaction times. It rules the majority of our unconscious mental processes such as walking, driving a car, making coffee in the morning, reacting when somebody insults us during the day and many more. Since safety is the mammal brain's main goal, it constantly tracks potential dangers and prefers us to stick to our current habits since they have resulted in our survival up to this point. If threatened, the mammal brain creates emotions we don't like, such as anxiety, fear or anger, to steer us away from danger or to get us back to the same old routines. The mammal brain's job is to keep us safe and save energy, and so it creates and maintains very powerful neural networks, which in turn automate our behaviour by creating habits. The mammal brain learns by repetition, creating the strongest brain networks for the actions we repeat most often. These are the crucial centres for what we call the unconscious mind, and all other mammals have similar centres too.

If we want to change our habits, we need to use another brain region – the neocortex (or the human brain), especially the very front part of it, called the prefrontal cortex (PFC for short). The neocortex is the largest part of the brain and is more developed than in any other animal, hence it is called the human brain. This structure is divided into many parts, each responsible for different functions. We will meet some of these centres in the next chapter since they are crucial for how we perceive the world and act in it. But just to give you a quick summary: the frontal lobes enable rational thinking and voluntary movements, the parietal lobes sense touch, temperature and taste, the occipital lobes are responsible for vision, and the temporal lobes control hearing and smell.

In terms of changing habits, the most crucial structure is at the very front of the frontal lobes, hence its name, the prefrontal cortex. The PFC is involved in a wide range of mental abilities which enable us to get things done throughout the day – the so-called executive functions of the brain: rational thinking, troubleshooting, analysing data, reasoning, learning new information, rational decision-making, creativity and many more. So pretty much everything we call rational intelligence. The PFC is also crucial for deciding what changes we want to create in our lives and it enables us to make these changes happen. The PFC is also the main area governing willpower, creating the ability to delay gratification and wait for long-term rewards, resisting temptations on the way.

The brain has a system of priorities when it comes to 'feeding' these different parts, which consume different amounts of energy. The lizard brain is the most efficient, and the human brain is the most energy consuming since it is responsible for complex functions that need the activity of thousands of neurons, requiring lots of glucose and oxygen to 'feed' them.

Let me use the metaphor of different motor vehicles to illustrate the difference in energy consumption of these centres. The lizard brain is like a small motorcycle – it is always on and it uses energy very efficiently, thus the brain always finds nutrients and oxygen for our lizard brain since if it didn't we would die. The mammal brain is like a light car – it's a lot more expensive fuel-wise than the lizard brain, but is still active for most of our waking hours, controlling our automatic habits. Some centres of the mammal brain are also active during sleep to process the information we encounter during the day. Last but not least, the human brain is like a plane – it uses enormous amounts of nutrients and oxygen, thus is active only when two conditions are met: first, when we are carrying out tasks which require these functions and second, when the brain has enough fuel left after feeding the other two brain centres. What this implies is that at the end of the day, when we are tired, and especially if we have been stressed, there is not enough energy for the human brain, particularly its most complex parts such as the PFC, to function optimally. For this very reason, we revert to old habits, which are governed by the more energy-efficient mammal brain. Therefore, if we want to start new habits, waiting until the end of the day is a bad idea. Our willpower (also governed by the PFC) is at its lowest at that point too. This phenomenon is called ego depletion. Willpower and other important qualities of the PFC are compromised at the end of the day when the brain has little energy left and the PFC needs time off. As a result, we are more prone to give in to temptations or choose whatever path is easiest. So, doing things in new ways requires us to use the more developed centres of the brain, for which a lot more energy is needed. Therefore, the first rule for creating new habits is to do new things either in the morning or straight after a break.

The habit loop – why bad habits are also good

Every habit we have developed over time meets certain needs. That also applies to 'bad habits'. We all need to meet lots of different needs. Some of them are physiological, such as hunger, thirst, sexual desire and so on. Others are psychological, such as safety/ stability, variety/novelty, connection/love, significance, growth/ learning and contribution to others. All of our actions, thoughts and emotional patterns have developed to meet these needs.

Let's come back to Andrew. The habit he hates the most is overeating sugary snacks, but that meets many of his physical and psychological needs. In the morning, he is hungry so a muffin eases that hunger. Also, due to a lack of sleep, he is often still really tired at the start of the day, therefore a sugar rush, especially with a strong coffee, provides him with a buzz of energy and short-term wakefulness. Moreover, sugar helps him to temporarily reduce his constant anxiety and gives him a short-lived feeling of safety and peace. Andrew's closest colleagues also live similar lifestyles so he often has an afternoon cup of coffee and another pastry with it, in that way meeting his need for connection.

As we can see, changing long-standing habits is often tricky as they do help us meet very important needs in pretty efficient ways. Such a simple thing as eating pastries allows Andrew to satisfy the needs of hunger, wakefulness, safety and connection. If Andrew wants to stop eating pastries, he first needs to find better ways to meet these needs. In addition, habits follow a so-called habit loop, which consists of a trigger (also called a cue), which can be the place, the time of day, the people, actions beforehand or a certain physical or emotional state. In this example, the trigger is the place: the coffee shop at the train station or the canteen at Andrew's work. Then follows the action: eating the pastry. And last but not least, the immediate reward, which is the specific needs I have mentioned such as reducing hunger and getting an energy boost. To change the habit, we need to keep the same cue and the same rewards, but replace the action with other ways of meeting these needs. For example, Andrew could meet the need to reduce hunger and get an energy boost (rewards) by having breakfast in the morning and having a small granola bar or healthy juice with his coffee (new actions) at the station (cue).

If we want to change our habits, we first need to choose one habit and make an honest inventory of what need this habit is meeting and what other ways there could be to meet these needs. This is one of the main reasons why simply stopping 'bad habits' doesn't work – the needs we fulfil with our bad habits are crucial and unless we offer a compelling alternative, we will have an enormous drive to revert to that habit once our willpower wears out.

Reward or pain – why do you want to change?

We naturally tend to be drawn to the things that cause us pleasure and try to avoid things that evoke pain. The parts of the brain you have to blame for that are reward and pain centres deep within the mammal brain. These reward centres secrete a neurotransmitter called dopamine, which creates a feeling of pleasure and motivation in an area of the brain called the nucleus accumbens (NAcc). Other centres of the brain such as the rational prefrontal cortex (PFC), the memory-holding hippocampus and the emotional amygdala are also connected to the NAcc, so they too can increase or decrease the levels of pleasure we experience with the judgements they make.

Imagine you are eating a delicious dinner and loads of dopamine molecules are 'tickling' your NAcc as you bite into an amazing Florentine steak (mmm…). Suddenly, you get a call to tell you that somebody in your family is ill, or your boss calls to give you some bad news on the project you were working on. How is your dinner now? The PFC has made a calculation about what this news means, using some facts taken from the hippocampus's library of memories and triggering relevant emotions in the amygdala. Anxiety, fear, stress and shock can completely block the satisfaction of even the greatest pleasures.

The opposite can happen too – the PFC's positive expectations can boost the sensation of pleasure. Imagine that you are in a Michelin-starred restaurant. You have been waiting for this day for so long! Finally, it is here! And what is this? Waiters dressed in white tuxedos bring huge plates with small blobs of red mash. You have no idea what the food is, but you take a bite of it on the end of the spoon and you expect nothing but total delicious-ness. And it is indeed delicious, partly because of all the amazing combinations of flavours, and partly because your PFC has been expecting it and has amplified the pleasure even more.

Emotional pain and fear centres are another part of the story. The main area for these is the amygdala, which keeps track of all the things that might have caused you damage in the past. However, the amygdala, being part of the mammal brain, is relatively primitive and often looks at the immediate consequences rather than long-term effects. The same applies for the reward centres of the brain, namely the areas called nucleus accumbens (NAcc) and the ventral tegmental area (VTA), which create the feeling of pleasure. For example, the delicious creamy pastry you might have for afternoon tea today will definitely give you a big dopamine kick, causing pleasure and a desire to do it again. A few hours later you might feel sluggish and have difficulty focusing on the task at hand, but the mammal brain centres might not have linked it to the coffee and sugary snack you had before. As a daily habit, long term this can cause weight gain, loss of productivity and type II diabetes, with the gruesome possibility of losing your toes, as well as brain and body inflammation – loads of unpleasant, health-threatening consequences. Doesn't sound good, does it? But does your mammal brain want to think about that? Of course not! And that's why we need to use our powerful rational PFC!

First, we have to come up with a list of as many benefits of changing that habit as we can and another list of negative consequences now and in the long term if we don't change it. Let's take replacing sugary snacks with healthier options as a desired change. We are aiming to write down around 50 benefits of the new behaviour and 50 drawbacks of being stuck in the old pattern to reinforce our motivation to change. To come up with such a large number of benefits and drawbacks for the new and the old behaviour, think of eight main areas of your life such as work, family, romantic relationship, social life, hobbies, physical health, mental health and personal growth or spiritual practices. Now go through each of these areas one by one and come up with as many benefits of the new behaviours and as many drawbacks of the old as you can for each of them. It might be helpful to take an A4 piece of paper, draw one vertical line in the middle and three equally spaced horizontal lines crossing it. That would divide the paper into eight equal squares. Dedicate each square to a different area of your life and label the squares. Draw a '+' on the left of each square and write as many benefits as you can think of for replacing sugary snacks with healthier options. For example, in the area of work, reducing sugar intake would mean: 1) a sharper focus on work; 2) fewer breaks for snacks; 3) looking better in a smart outfit; 4) feeling more confident in your own looks when meeting new clients; 5) maybe fewer migraines; 6) less brain fog. Draw a '–' sign on the right part of the square and write down all the drawbacks of eating two to three sugary snacks a day at work: 1) feeling sluggish after a while, then drinking too much coffee, which makes you jittery and it gets hard to focus on the task; 2) constantly craving more sugary snacks, taking your attention away from the task; 3) gaining weight and so needing to buy larger clothes for work, which is costly; 4) feeling a bit embarrassed around colleagues due to your unhealthy diet; 5) snacking so much causes you to skip main meals, which sometimes triggers a migraine; 6) feeling that it contributes negatively to productivity overall and makes you procrastinate more.

Now if you extend this to the other seven areas, you will end up with around 50 benefits and 50 drawbacks. You can also find more examples in the lists Andrew came up with to change his habits in the summary of this chapter.

In other words, we need to retrain our mammal brain's pleasure and pain centres in what habits actually mean long term – will they get us where we want to go or will they get in the way? It is important to remember that your mammal brain will forget these associations and will seek immediate gratification, so it's best to keep these lists somewhere visible to keep reminding your mammal brain of the long-term consequences.

The other option is to have an even stronger long-term reward to motivate you to overcome the immediate gratifications or to make short-term rewards harder to access. You may have come across the marshmallow test (Michel et al., 1989). A bunch of four-year-olds were asked to sit in a room with a marshmallow on the table. They were told that if they waited until the researcher came back and resisted eating the treat, they would get two marshmallows afterwards. Not surprisingly, many four-year-olds couldn't wait and chose one marshmallow now instead of two later. However, some of them managed to resist the temptation and were rewarded with a bigger treat. When researchers followed the performance of these kids, the second group had higher test scores at school and ended up in better jobs earning significantly larger salaries. What does this experiment tell us? Some of us have more impulsive natures and lean towards short-term gratification rather than long-term gain. This group might have beautiful dreams for the future but when faced with the temptation of sugary snacks, online shopping and easy access to social media, future dreams will be temporarily pushed aside and will carry little weight in the decision-making process. If you are one of these people, you might consider making quick rewards harder: cancel Amazon Prime, keep your phone in a desk drawer or in another room, cancel your credit cards, create an automatic transfer to your savings account, get rid of all the junk food at home.

But no matter how good we are at impulse control, having a lack of clarity in terms of long-term direction can still get us lost in short-term temptations. If you are particularly prone to impulsive behaviour, try to be as clear as possible about how you would like your life to be in five or ten years. What would you like to do? What would you like to look like and feel like? How much money would you like to earn and have in your savings account? What kind of relationship or family would you like to have? What experiences would you like to have and who would you like to share them with? The more vividly we can imagine the future we are trying to build, the more it stimulates our reward centres and the easier it is to resist the habits that get in the way.

When emotions switch off the rational brain

Although we'll discuss the importance and meaning of emotions in the next chapter, we need to touch on them here. Imagine your boss has just treated you unfairly and now you feel raging anger. Maybe you see your girlfriend flirting with a very good-looking man and you suddenly get an overwhelming sense of jealousy. Or you are waiting for an important job interview and you feel so much anxiety that it's getting hard to breathe and your heart is pounding so loudly that you fear everyone in the room can hear it. Have you ever experienced anything like that? If so, have you said something or done something in that situation that you have regretted afterwards? If you are like most of us, the answer is most likely to be yes. And that's OK; it means your brain is functioning exactly as it should!

You see, the neurons in the amygdala are connected to neurons in the PFC. When the amygdala is activated by real or imaginary dangers it can temporarily 'switch off' the part of the PFC called the ventromedial PFC (vmPFC), making sound rational decisions physically impossible at that moment. This phenomenon is called the amygdala hijack of the PFC and usually lasts about 20–30 minutes, but the most intense phase is just a few minutes long. The worst thing is that in that situation we don't realise that we are out of order since we need our PFC to give us perspective, which is unfortunately temporarily compromised at that moment. So, when we change anything in our lives, it is usually best to avoid causing that amygdala hijack if possible. Activities such as journal writing, meditation, physical exercise, time with people whose company is soothing, cuddling pets, or hugs with loved ones also reduce any lingering background activity in the amygdala and make it less likely to accumulate into strong emotions.

So, if we want to successfully change our habits we need to keep our mammal brains feeling safe. We can do that with amygdala-soothing activities and by implementing change in small steps, maintaining the feeling of familiarity. Also, whenever possible, it is best to change one thing at a time. Creating loads of New Year's resolutions with ambitious big changes is in fact the worst thing you can do for your amygdala. Instead, ask yourself these questions:

- What one thing would I like to change this month?
- What could I do this week towards it?
- What small step could I take this week to make this action possible?

For example, if I want to prioritise sorting out my finances this month, I might choose to look at my bank statements during the first week. Then when the next week comes, I might want to look at which of my cards have the highest rates and redistribute my credit accordingly. The week after I might schedule a meeting with a financial advisor. The week after that I might ask my bank to start an automated saving programme by taking 10 per cent of my salary each month. This way your PFC doesn't get overwhelmed by the number of tasks to deal with and the amygdala has only one new thing each week so it doesn't feel threatened.

New habits – new networks

So how do we actually change? First of all, each skill, thought, emotion and character trait in your brain is encoded in the form of a neural network. A neural network is just a group of neurons in various areas of your brain connected with each other and 'communicating' via small electrical currents called nervous impulses. That's right, every thought you have is created by small currents of electricity in your brain. However, different networks produce different thoughts and the ones we use more get stronger and stronger over time. The opposite is true as well – the networks we don't use as much get weaker and weaker over time and might disappear altogether. That's how we forget things – the networks storing that memory or skill get so weak that we can't recreate the initial information. That phenomenon is called activity-dependent plasticity and is why the brain is often compared to a muscle in a 'use it or lose it' manner. And although the mechanisms by which muscles get stronger and brain networks get more developed are completely different, the main principle of us being somewhat in charge of training them is similar.

If we want to develop new habits, we simply need to create new networks or strengthen the existing networks until they become so strong that the habit is automatic. So how do we create new networks and is it possible to do that at all when we are in our thirties, forties, fifties or even eighties and beyond? The answer is yes and no. Neuroplasticity is by definition a flexible process – the more we surround ourselves with new information, the more plastic our brains become. However, if we do exactly the same things each and every day, our brains get a bit rusty and might take a little training to get back to learning mode. However, it is never too late – the brain is capable of change throughout life and every time we undergo change, plasticity is enhanced.

Learning is a very costly process, which takes a lot of brain resources, energy and time, thus we only develop new networks if we really need to. How long does it take to form new habits? There is no simple answer to that. It depends on the skill, the experience you have and how often you do it. First, different skills require different numbers of neural networks to be formed, so a more complex change, such as starting a completely new job, would require thousands of new networks. Second, if you have already done something before, the networks might still be there but weakened through lack of use, so strengthening them is a less costly process than creating something from scratch – for example, refreshing the French you learned at school as opposed to learning an unfamiliar foreign language. Last but not least, the more often you use a skill, the quicker you will build it. At the start of learning there is a temporary plasticity, which diminishes if there is no repetition; however, if the action is repeated the next day or multiple times a day, that temporary plasticity eventually becomes the longer-term strengthening of the network and the skill becomes more automatic. So when we start a new activity we must be prepared that it will take at least a month or two for it to become automatic. For that reason, we need to surround ourselves with a necessary level of support to keep on maintaining that new habit even if it would be easier just to drop it and go back to the old familiar ways when the going gets rough.

Summary of Chapter One

Let's come back to Andrew. If he wants to change his life, he first needs to choose one area and one habit to start with. Let's say he wants to start with eating more healthily in the mornings. Let's look at what he is currently occupying his mornings with – he wakes up, checks his emails and messages on the work phone, gets stressed out, jumps in the shower, gets dressed and leaves for work. Now that is already a stressful morning.

Imagine if he left his work phone at work and did not sync his work emails to his personal phone. That would already create some separation between work and home. Once he wakes up, he might start the day with a protein-based breakfast such as scrambled egg, or boiled egg with a cup of green tea, to gently wake him up. It's best for him personally to eat before showering, as that's when his thinking about work starts, followed by growing levels of anxiety, killing his appetite and making him feel he must urgently leave for work. By contrast, if he jumps in the shower after breakfast, some food in his system will already have triggered his parasympathetic nervous system (also called rest and digest) which has a calming effect on the stress response, so he won't get as anxious as he used to. He gets dressed and takes a train to central London.

Once Andrew arrives at the train station, he might skip the coffee shop altogether and get coffee at work, or he might grab black coffee and an apple if he really wants to keep the habit of an energising kick when he arrives. Would Andrew be resistant to starting this habit? Almost certainly yes, and perhaps the hardest part for him would be leaving his phone at work. So what he needs to do before he starts to implement this change is to sit down and make a list of the benefits now and in the future of leaving his phone at work. He needs to get a clear idea of how this new habit will alter, for the better, all areas of his life: his health and fitness, mental wellbeing, work performance and his career path in general, hobbies, financial situation, family relationships, social life and even his intimate life with his wife. We are not looking at the pros and cons at this stage, as that would just keep him stuck. We are looking just at the pros of a new habit. Also, it is important to choose just one habit at a time as we want to build positive associations with specific actions, otherwise it is too vague for the brain. For example, we all know that most of us could do with eating more healthily, but that phrase doesn't mean much to the brain. However, if we replace it with swapping pain au chocolat for porridge with berries and banana three times a week, that becomes something the brain can execute.

Andrew's list of reasons for leaving his work phone at work could look something like this:

1. *Family:* I will no longer work in the evenings, so I will have more time to spend with my wife and kids. I could perhaps cook them a nice meal. I could help my eight-year-old daughter with her Spanish, and take her to programming club or swimming classes to gradually rebuild our bond. I would also have more time to play with my five-year-old son.

2. *Health and fitness:* I will move around more and might even have time to do some exercise or walk an extra block from the train station. I will no longer feel so anxious so might not need to snack on sugary treats as much to calm me down. I will also have more time to do some exercise with my kids over the weekends.

3. *Mental health:* I will finally start to reduce my levels of anxiety and stress and that may well help with my depressive episodes too. My mind will feel sharper as my brain will have enough time to recover and replenish the nutrients and neurotransmitters (we will talk about that in the next chapters).

4. *Work performance and career path:* If I separate work and rest I will finally be able to have some recovery time and feel much fresher the next day. Also, I will probably start missing my work so I will look forward to it. Moreover, I will have more time to process ideas so I might come up with better solutions and more creative approaches. Given that my PFC will be greatly recovered, my work performance will improve almost immediately. I will also be in a better mood the next day so my colleagues will find me much more fun to be around. Most importantly, I will have more space in my mind to focus on the needs of my team members and be a better leader for them.

5. *Finances:* Being a better performer at work, I will get bigger bonuses. Also, I will have more time to look at my finances and think how best to invest our savings. I will be more

on top of things, so will not run into big credit card fees or other unnecessary payments. Also, being more relaxed and less anxious, I will be doing less impulsive online shopping for gadgets and have time to consider what it is that we really need.

6. *Social life:* I will finally have time to meet up with my old friends. I will feel more relaxed around people and stop checking my phone as often, which I know some of my friends find very disrespectful. I will be able to be more present around them and be there for them more. With improved relationships, I might start feeling more comfortable about sharing my problems, so might start feeling less isolated.

7. *Hobbies:* I will finally have time to watch movies, play squash and experiment with cooking recipes. In fact, I can't wait to do that! I was so wrapped up in my work that I no longer allowed myself to do other things I used to truly enjoy.

8. *Emotional and physical intimacy with my wife:* I will be able to be there for my wife more. I will be a better listener and less preoccupied with reacting to my work emails and unresolved problems at work. I will show her more attention: cook meals, buy flowers, figure out what things she likes so I can get her amazing birthday and Christmas gifts or just buy little tokens without any occasion. I will have time to take better care of my physical appearance and with having more than just work going for me, she might start finding me more attractive again.

Of course, we can keep going. The more reasons you can come up with, the stronger positive associations you will build. This will secrete more dopamine in the reward system of your brain, naturally increasing your levels of motivation to make a change.

OK, so Andrew has now identified that he could create some space in the evenings and in the mornings simply by leaving his work phone at work. Then he came up with a list of reasons why he needs to do that. Now he must identify what needs he is meeting by constantly checking his work phone and what the triggers are for him to do so.

For one week, Andrew has been noting when he was checking his phone out of work hours. What was he doing? How was he feeling? What happened before? Who was he with? What did he need to do afterwards? By doing this written audit, he has identified that his main trigger is emotional – anxiety – so the reward in this habit is a changed emotional state or a distraction from anxiety. Then he works with his coach to identify what other things could help him to reduce anxiety. In his case, breathing exercises, listening to Headspace meditations and writing a journal seem to work pretty well. So he starts developing new ways to meet his needs. At this point, he is still bringing his phone back home, but every time he feels a desire to check it, he needs to do a five-minute breathing exercise before he is allowed to do so. Interestingly, most of the time, the need to check his phone is greatly reduced after the breathing exercise.

Then Andrew decides on his first small step – leaving the phone at work one day a week (Monday). To get some reassurance, he speaks to his line manager and shares his problems with anxiety and tells him about the programme he is working on with his coach to deal with it. His line manager, of course, agrees that he is not expected to take his phone home and that he is only required to be available during working hours. He also shares with Andrew that he himself comes to work one hour earlier, before the office gets busy, so he has time to reply to important emails before he starts getting distracted by his team. Andrew likes that idea and decides to start coming to work at 8 a.m. on Tuesdays rather than 9 a.m. after leaving his phone there on Monday nights. That helps Andrew to deal with his fear that he might not have enough time to reply to work emails during the day. Having successfully completed this task three times, Andrew rewards himself by buying new shoes, which he has wanted to do for a while but didn't feel worthy of.

The last step is creating a long-term plan and getting long-term support. Well, Andrew has already taken care of that – he has told his boss and his wife that this is what he wants to do and they both promised to keep him accountable to it. Also, he is having a weekly coaching session where he is able to share any obstacles with his coach and have time and space to troubleshoot them. He has a long-term reward waiting for him – a holiday in Tuscany with his wife and children at the end of a three-month period if he sticks to his plan.

To change habits, we need to go through these stages:

1. To enable change, we need to manage the energy levels of the prefrontal cortex, which gets tired and overloaded easily. We can achieve this by reducing mental load, prioritising tasks and doing any new actions first thing in the morning or after a break.

2. To increase our motivation, we need to activate the reward centres of the brain. We can do that by writing a list of benefits the new habit would give us now and in the future in all areas of life (be as specific as you can and include the most meaningful subjects for you).

3. We cannot get rid of bad habits easily as they help us to meet vital needs for our brains. We first need to identify which specific need this habit is meeting and then replace it with other habits which meet the exact same need.

4. The amygdala, the ancient emotional centre of the mammal part of the brain, hates novelty and gets easily scared if we change too much too quickly. When we feel freaked out, our amygdala creates high levels of anxiety, anger and other emotions we hate, and can even temporarily block our PFC, creating impulsive behaviours we often regret afterwards.

Doing amygdala-soothing activities such as walking, meditation, or spending time with loved ones keeps our anxiety levels lower and reduces the risk of amygdala hijack.

5. To create new habits we need to create new brain networks and strengthen them. That, unfortunately, takes time, energy and repetition. The brain will only keep new networks if they are being used often enough (that's why it is called activity-dependent plasticity), thus, small and often is a much more effective way to create new habits than lots every now and then. When creating a new habit, we have to create a strategy for how we will keep it for at least two months – social accountability, writing a journal, having long-term rewards, getting a support team if needed.

CHAPTER TWO

Changing Your Emotions

In this chapter, you will learn:

- The eight main types of emotion and their purpose.
- Where in the brain emotions are produced.
- What happens in the brain when we are overwhelmed by anger, anxiety or sadness, and how this changes our cognitive abilities.
- Practical tips on how to soothe our brains when we are getting overwhelmed.
- A few ways to challenge our emotional patterns using our rational mind.

An emotional component is vital for our wellbeing and personal fulfilment, but feeling anxiety, stress or fear can ruin even the best experiences. We now know that the daily and life choices we make, from what food we eat to who we choose to date or what jobs we take, are largely affected by our emotions, no matter how rational we think we are. Emotions carry valuable information about our internal and external environment – and yet emotions are a topic we rarely talk about and don't have much understanding of. The positive affirmations movement has backfired in this area by teaching us to suppress unpleasant emotions and pump ourselves up with positive thoughts. Unfortunately, 'positive thinking' makes us even less aware of our true feelings about events, with the result that we often make bad decisions, lose true happiness and even become depressed.

In this chapter, I will explain the real nature and importance of emotions, what happens in the brain when you experience them and how to let them guide you into making the best choices for you. Moreover, you will learn why we make very poor judgements under intense emotional pressures such as stress and anxiety and how best to deal with these situations. By the end of this chapter, you will be able to understand the emotional messages vital for sound decision-making and have practical tools to help regulate your emotional patterns.

Evolutionary role of emotions

Let me take you back 10,000 years to visit the place where it all began – the African savannah. Humans lived in hunter-gatherer communities with a clear goal – the survival of individuals and the species. The conditions were fierce – no fridges, no TV, no smartphones, no online food deliveries (imagine that)! Humans, not dissimilarly from many other mammals, had to hunt prey or gather the goods they could find. Moreover, they had to avoid being hunted by other species and that required very agile brains and bodies to immediately react to the environment. Getting distracted or being too optimistic could have made the difference between bringing home lunch or becoming somebody else's lunch. What processes in our brains have ensured our survival?

To survive, we needed a really quick detection system, not only to alert us to the danger, but also to change the physiology of the body to react to danger appropriately (usually to run away or to fight – the fight or flight response). And that's how our mammal brain parts (or the limbic system) came in really handy – nearly instantaneous threat detection by the amygdala was followed by automatic habitual responses to ensure survival.

Human emotions produced by the mammal brain centres enable us to make snap judgements about the environment, increasing our chances of survival. Even though our environment has evolved, the emotional centres of the brain have not changed. In order to understand the emotional meaning behind our patterns of behaviour, we must take the role they served in evolution into account.

All human emotions can be clustered into eight major groups: sadness, anger, guilt/shame, disgust, fear, surprise, excitement/joy, love/trust. Each of these different emotions has a distinct purpose and specific triggers associated with it. The trigger is followed by the physiological body response to elicit behaviour which will aid the survival of the individual and/or the species. However, due to a big shift in our living conditions, a lot of triggers are imaginary and the behavioural responses we engage in (like eating chocolate chip cookies when sad) do not necessarily increase our likelihood of survival. Thus, when looking at each type of emotion, we will address which responses are beneficial and which ones are counterproductive.

Trigger → Emotion → Physiological changes → Behaviour → Survival of individual/species

Eight types of human emotions

1. Sadness

Sadness is a passive emotion in response to a situation that is not good for you. Sadness can be triggered by a loved one leaving you, the illness you cannot do anything about or being stuck in a job you hate but feel powerless to change. There is always a certain level of lack of control when we feel sadness. It reduces the blood flow to the muscles and creates a sense of weakness, and a feeling of wanting to give up. This powerlessness can be real or perceived; the mammal brain centres do not know the difference. When we feel sad we might engage in behaviours to escape that unpleasant feeling – eating chocolate, watching funny YouTube videos, drinking alcohol or immersing ourselves in exercise or work. This is called escapism. In certain situations, of course, escapism is needed to regulate the intensity of the feelings and give our bodies a chance to recover and replenish themselves. However, if we engage in escapism behaviours on a frequent basis, that leads to addictive habits. If we constantly accumulate feelings we are trying to run away from, that will require stronger distractions, leading to serious addictions we might truly struggle to break. I will address how to deal with those later on. Let's get back to sadness. What could be a useful response when we feel sadness? It depends on the situation, of course. Let's take Lucy, who hates her job. Every Monday she goes to work and feels truly sad before she even gets there. If her work situation is a trigger of that sadness, we need to look at what it is specifically about her job that is creating that level of disempowerment. One exercise I like to do with my career-coaching clients is the career values tool. For that you need to write down eight main criteria of your dream job. Let's not get attached to the job roles here, but just imagine what things need to be in place for you to be happy in your job. Lucy came up with this list:

- Significance – being acknowledged for the work.
- Autonomy – having freedom to make decisions.
- Freedom of time and location – being able to work flexible hours and sometimes work from home too.
- Mentoring people – helping others grow.
- Finances – earning £50–60,000 a year.
- Contribution – making a positive impact on the world.

- Encouraging team – belonging to a supportive group.
- Empowering leadership – having a mentor who believes in me.

Then I asked Lucy to rate each of these aspects in her current job (1–10, with 1 being not at all good and 10 being amazing). Lucy thought for a moment and came up with this assessment:

- Significance – 9
- Autonomy – 8
- Freedom of time and location – 9
- Mentoring people – 4
- Finances – 10
- Contribution – 3
- Encouraging team – 3
- Empowering leadership – 2

OK, now we have a better picture – Lucy is a very high achiever in a high status role. She is well paid and has lots of freedom and autonomy. However, she lacks human contact and doesn't feel that she fits in with the rest of the team. She barely sees her line manager and she spends most of her time in front of her computer. Moreover, Lucy doubts that her job makes any valuable contribution to society. Her sadness is telling her that despite being unfulfilled, she receives too many positive things from her job and therefore she doesn't want to leave it but she doesn't know how to fix her situation. She feels powerless and the behaviour she engages in when feeling this way is eating sugary snacks and browsing social media. That doesn't fix the situation though and is starting to affect her wellbeing and work performance, causing her to stall even more. What actions could help her to get unstuck? Lucy could seek out books on career change. She could also join a community of other people going through the same experience.

Moreover, she could work with a coach to help her get unstuck. She could also evaluate her transferable skills and look for a job in a different industry or maybe seek out opportunities to change her department within the same company in order to address some of the things she has been lacking in her current role. The options are endless. However, sadness paralyses our thinking (we will discuss the mechanisms of it later on), causing us to be stuck in inaction, especially if the gap between where we are and where we want to be seems huge.

2. Anger

The second emotion is *anger*. In contrast to sadness, anger is an active emotion as a response to real or perceived danger. Anger pumps the muscles of our limbs with oxygen-rich blood and makes our heart beat fast to prepare us to run away from unkind situations or fight our way through them. As with sadness, there is usually a clear trigger to set it off and repeated usage of that response becomes stronger and easier to elicit. Triggers of anger are individual and are often set early in life, depending on our childhood and upbringing. Frequent triggers involve situations that can cause harm to us or to people we care about. The other group of triggers are social – it's very common to feel anger due to unfairness, being misunderstood or ignored, overly criticised, not getting enough attention or generally not getting your needs met sufficiently in your relationships. Interestingly, the same situation for some people can cause anger while for others it can cause sadness. Let's imagine that Lucy, who we mentioned before, had a slightly different take on her situation – she might realise that she should have much more support from her line manager. She feels anger over the lack of response to her emails from her manager. Personal temperament and perceived level of control during childhood and later in life could influence whether a person reacts to situations with anger or sadness. Another factor in this reaction is the perceived cause (whether we blame ourselves or somebody else for the situation), which brings me to the next set of emotions – guilt and shame.

3. Guilt and shame

Guilt and shame are social emotions to indicate that your actions or way of being don't fit in with society's needs. Guilt is often triggered by something we have done but we think we shouldn't (or something we have not done but we think we should). In evolutionary terms, this emotion indicated that you were not pulling your weight in your tribe and whether your actions endangered the coherence of the group. It was a feedback mechanism to steer behaviour back on track to what was beneficial for the group. In modern times though, the main triggers of guilt are 'shoulds' – internalised guidelines from other people or societal expectations we think we should meet. Whenever we feel that emotion, we must examine our thinking. To do so, please make an extensive list of all the 'shoulds' you can think of. It can be in any area of your life, such as your status, job, body, health – anything you criticise yourself over.

When I asked Lucy about hers, here is the list she came up with:

- I should own a house in London.
- I should earn a six-figure salary.
- I should have children and be a dedicated mum.
- I should marry and have an amazing relationship, which lasts forever.
- I should go to the gym every day.
- I should never be angry.
- I should have lots of friends and go out with them often.

- I should cook my own meals.
- I should be slim and fit.
- I should stop eating junk food.
- I should not drink as much coffee as I do now.
- I should wake up earlier to meditate or go for a run.
- I should keep my flat neater.
- I should call my family more.
- I should travel more.
- I should help others more.
- I should not get so tired in the evenings.
- I should not be grumpy with my boyfriend.
- I should not be as needy with him.
- I should save more money.

Write as many 'shoulds' as you can think of. Now, if you look at Lucy's list, there are a lot of unrealistic expectations – one group of 'shoulds' tells Lucy to focus on relationships, have kids and be a dedicated mother, while other 'shoulds' expect her to be career focused, earn lots of money and buy a house in London. Not surprisingly, Lucy feels stuck as she keeps 'failing' to live up to such standards. To address that, we first need to look at where these beliefs came from and whether they truly matter to Lucy at this stage of her life. We accumulate a lot of 'shoulds' from parental and authority figures during childhood and later in life, internalising their values and their voices in our own thinking (we will discuss values in much greater detail in the chapter on personality). However, we can use our rational prefrontal cortex to challenge them and ask these questions:

1. Who do these 'shoulds' from my list belong to? (Go through each statement on the list and write down the name of the person or people who indoctrinated your thinking with

those beliefs either with advice they gave or the example
they set for you.)
2. On a scale of 1–10, how important is the topic mentioned
   in this statement for me personally at this stage in my life?
3. What would be the drawback of me following that 'should'?

This last question is trying to bring balance and realistic expectations to our thinking – given that we have a limited amount of
time, energy and other resources, we have to prioritise what we
use it for. When we focus on one area of life, we are neglecting
others. Empowering our life requires making a conscious choice
of what is truly important to us at a given moment in time and
shifting focus to that value. Looking at your 'should' that way
immediately brings a much more objective perspective to what
is and isn't possible. It helps you to remove the self-blame and
shame. It is important to note that guilt is an emotion directed at
specific actions or inactions while shame is directed at the object
being faulty to the core. Feeling shame indicates that there is a big
gap between a set of beliefs of what one should be and what one
really is. Not surprisingly, tackling shame requires a lot more work
and can be linked to childhood trauma, which we will discuss in
greater detail in Chapter Eight on relationships.

4. Disgust

The fourth emotion is *disgust*. In an evolutionary sense, it helped us
to stay away from objects that were not suitable to eat and people
who were potentially carrying dangerous illnesses. Our thinking
centres (the PFC in particular) are connected to mammal brain
centres, which create emotions, and therefore our moral beliefs
can trigger feelings of disgust as well. We often hear about people
feeling disgusted when they find out that their partner has been

cheating on them or read a news story about someone abusing vulnerable people, especially children. The disgust indicates that moral norms have been violated but there is not much we can do to set it right at that given moment.

5. Fear

The fifth emotion – *fear* – evolved to keep us away from situations where we had no chance to win (for example, much larger predators, severe weather conditions, big heights). Fear can also be triggered by imagining a future situation that would be harmful for our survival. Given the tendency of the mammal brain structures to emphasise danger, we often imagine a future being much worse than it really turns out to be. However, our mammal brain doesn't know the reality, it just believes the thoughts we have, creating strong emotional reactions to these thoughts as if they were real. Common triggers for fear include thoughts of loved ones leaving us, being diagnosed with a terminal illness, getting severely injured, going bankrupt, losing a job. Most of these things we fear don't really happen and even if they do, we often are much more equipped to deal with them than we thought we would be. Let's imagine Lucy fears losing her job. Given that she gets no input from her boss, there is no way of knowing if her performance is satisfactory or not. When I first asked Lucy what would happen if she did lose her job, her body tensed up and she went blank. Then I asked her to imagine a person (let's call him George) who was in a job he hated and felt unappreciated. What would be the benefits of George being made redundant? Lucy perked up and started to brainstorm ideas: he could find another job, he could use the pay-out to get trained in a completely different sector, he could travel and work in different countries teaching English, he could go to Hawaii and surf until the money runs out, he could move in with his parents for a while or live with his friends until he got an idea of what to do next. The options were endless. We looked at Lucy's situation next. She smiled and was now able to come up with lots of great scenarios of how she would use her time, energy and savings if she was made redundant – to the point that she almost started to wish for it! And that is not unusual – when we investigate the object of our fear, we realise that we have more options than we thought we did. If you have a persisting fear of some future event, I would suggest visiting that future land and brainstorming ideas as if it were about somebody else – that might open up new perspectives.

Another kind of fear is a phobia, a very primal reaction to situations that would have been deadly if we hadn't developed modern tools (e.g. fear of flying, fear of snakes). To address phobias, we need to find a way to communicate safety to our amygdala, which is not easy to do when it is raging. But we shall talk more about that later in this chapter when we look at amygdala-soothing techniques.

6. *Surprise*

The sixth emotion – *surprise* – can either be a welcoming emotion or an unpleasant one, depending on the outcome. Surprise prepares the body to deal with the situation of uncertainty when the outcome is not yet known. If Lucy came back home and saw a bucket of flowers by the door, she would feel surprise first before she knew whether to feel excited about a date opportunity with somebody she liked, or to freak out if it was from somebody in whom she had no romantic interest.

The last two types of emotions are what we call positive emotions: excitement/joy and love/trust. They both indicate that the situation we are in or the activities we are engaged in are good for our survival or the survival of the species.

7. Excitement and joy

Common triggers for *excitement/joy* are fun times with family or friends (indicates good group cohesion), doing activities that we prefer (indicates that the world is safe enough to focus on these things), delicious food (physical survival), being on a date with a person we find very attractive (survival of the species… hehe). Of course, sometimes our mammal brain and human brain centres disagree – sugary snacks and putting on fat might prepare your body for survival but won't make you look as good as you would like to on the beach. Or that person your body is so desperately attracted to might be a psycho you don't want anything to do with (or you might be in a relationship with somebody else). So, yes, that can get a bit complicated.

8. Love and trust

Last, but not least, *love and trust* are social emotions (which I'll group together as one emotion) we develop if we have enough safety and predictability in our relationship with another person. This emotion has evolved to keep parents looking after their offspring and to encourage partners to come back to each other. For love and trust to last, predictability in behaviour is needed. Trust, in particular, is very hard to recover after the incidents that are not congruent with previous behaviours (such as lying). We shall visit the topic of love in Chapter Eight on relationships.

As you can see, there are five emotions to warn us about real or perceived danger and only two to signal that things are going well (surprise can fall either way, depending on the outcome). This unfair distribution indicates that it is much more important for us to avoid danger than to seek pleasure, creating a bias towards noticing negative things. That is not only OK, but also, it is a very clever design that kept our species safe and sound over thousands of years. Let's look now at what happens in the body and brain to mediate these responses and assess if there is anything we can do about them.

Emotional systems in the brain and body

To accurately feel emotions, we need the following components:

1. *Threat detector* – a system that detects levels of danger in the environment and triggers specific danger-related emotions. The ancient mammal brain structure, the amygdala, working as a threat detector, accurately and very quickly detects danger.

2. *Pleasure detector* – a system, also called the *reward system*, that has evolved to detect objects and people in the environment that could be beneficial for our survival and the survival of our species. It consists of the ventral tegmental area (VTA), which detects the potential for pleasure in the environment, and the nucleus accumbens (Nacc), which creates the feeling of pleasure when we eat delicious food, engage in mating behaviours or read a fascinating book.

3. *Brain–body connector* – a system that influences different body parts to prepare for different emotions. A brain structure called the *hypothalamus* connects the brain with the body by secreting hormones that trigger certain states and behaviours to maintain the homeostasis, a process by which we maintain stability in our body. Also, it serves to some extent as a body–brain connector – the hypothalamus is constantly monitoring the state of your blood and the levels of glucose.

4. *Body–brain connector* – a system that reads our body states and adjusts our brain processes accordingly. Another brain part called the *insula* constantly monitors the body states

(also called visceral information) and adjusts the nervous system functioning accordingly. The insula detects an increased heart rate and fast breathing and in turn exacerbates the anxiety, creating a vicious cycle.

5. *Activator* – a system that activates all of the body organs into an arousal state if danger has been detected. This function is taken care of by the sympathetic nervous system (SNS), which is part of the autonomic nervous system (ANS), the system which controls the activity of all of the major body organs to prepare them for different states. The job of the SNS is to prepare the body to run away or to fight the danger (the fight or flight response). To do so, it first triggers the secretion of adrenalin (also called epinephrine) from your adrenal glands (at the top of your kidneys). Then it changes your breathing to quick and shallow, and the adrenalin makes your heart beat fast and stimulates the release of glucose into your bloodstream from your liver. Adrenalin also dilates your blood vessels in the muscles of your limbs, blocks the digestive and the immune systems and increases the threshold for pain. If the triggers are all in your mind, your brain keeps switching your body to a constant state of alertness, creating high blood pressure and shallow, fast breathing, blocking digestion (thus, causing stomach cramps or bowel problems) and the immune system (making us more vulnerable to infections). If these internal stressors are constantly present, your body doesn't get a chance to rest and replenish, giving rise to various physical and mental health issues.

6. *Soother* – a system that calms down the body's arousal after the danger is over or if pleasure has been detected. This is created by a second branch of the ANS, the parasympathetic nervous system (PSNS). Once the danger is over, the parasympathetic system kicks in to give the body a chance

to relax and replenish (called the 'rest and digest' state). The PSNS makes your breathing deep and slow, reduces the heartbeat to a much more peaceful pace and switches the digestion and immune systems back on. These mechanisms of PSNS and SNS are automatic and involuntary, meaning that we don't really have wilful control over them. The only part we can control to some extent is our breathing. Therefore, a lot of stress-calming techniques are based around changing the way we breathe.

7. *Learner* – a system that can make sense of what has happened and learn from the situation, and how to avoid the danger in future. The learner mainly consists of the prefrontal cortex (PFC), which assesses what has happened and is able to compare that experience to all the knowledge it has gained from past experiences to make meaning out of it. That learning allows for us to adapt and change. PFC functioning is affected, though, if our body is in a stressed state (sympathetic nervous system, SNS) or is replenishing (parasympathetic nervous system, PSNS). During the SNS state, there are not enough resources for fine PFC functioning, which compromises our learning and rational assessment. During the PSNS state, PFC blood vessels can dilate and provide plenty of oxygen and glucose for these centres to function. In that state, we are capable of learning effectively, understanding others and exhibiting empathy and compassion.

Changing emotional patterns by soothing the amygdala

When we talk about managing emotions, what we mean is soothing the amygdala, shifting the body from the sympathetic to the parasympathetic system and giving the body and brain chemistry a chance to recover. Only then we can expect clear thinking, creativity, the ability to connect and to be present for others. One of the quickest ways to achieve it is breathing. When we start to breathe deeply into the stomach and slow the breathing right down, especially the breathing-out phase, the insula learns that it must be safe out there (in other words, if you were running away from a predator you wouldn't have time for a slow breath out). This provides an opportunity to break that vicious cycle and for the body to switch, at least for a short period of time, to the parasympathetic nervous system (PSNS). Interestingly, these body states are self-perpetuating – when we are aroused we get a skewed perception of the world around us. An aroused state makes the amygdala more alert to danger. Not surprisingly, the amygdala finds more triggers and we perceive the world as a much more dangerous and negative place. In turn, when the amygdala is calm, our PFC is active, giving it a chance to see the world more objectively.

Breathing exercise

First breathe in through your nose to the count of four, hold to the count of four and breathe out to the count of four. We are aiming to prolong the breathing-out phase to allow the body to switch on the relaxation response, so if you can prolong it for a count of six or eight, that would be even better, but a count of four is enough. Find the pace that works for you. Close your eyes and do it four more times.

Now we can add some visualisation to take this further. When you are breathing in the next time, imagine it is sunny outside and you are breathing in that sunshine and light. Fill your stomach, chest and back as you inhale and feel how your whole body relaxes. Hold it for a little bit. And now breathe out slowly and gently. Next imagine you are by the sea and you can hear the waves crashing into the shore. Breathe in that freshness and freedom. Fill your stomach, chest and back, feel how your back straightens. Hold it. Now let your shoulders drop down, relaxing when you are breathing out slowly and gently. Now imagine it is wintertime. You are sitting by the fireplace with a blanket around your shoulders and a warm cup of tea in your hands and you are just watching the fire in the fireplace. Breathe in that warmth and coziness. Fill your stomach, chest and back, feel how your whole body fills with warmth. Breathe out slowly and gently. Now imagine there is a candle on the table. You are looking at the flame of the candle and you breathe in that peace and tranquility. Fill your stomach, chest and back, feel how your whole body relaxes. Now breathe out slowly and gently. How are you feeling?

When I guide people through this exercise in my seminars, most people share that they feel very calm and relaxed. Paying attention to the breathing and particularly slowing down and switching to the parasympathetic system allows our bodies and brains to replenish. Pleasant visualisation helps to keep our minds busy with something that does not trigger the amygdala's danger detection (if we allow our mind to wander it usually finds things to worry about, which can interfere with breathing or meditative practices, especially if we are new to it or if we are going through a rough patch).

Movement

Another way to change the physiological response of the body is movement. The insula keeps reading what your body is doing, and ancient slow movement practices such as yoga and tai chi communicate safety to your brain. Other kinds of exercise such as rock climbing, cycling or jogging can help to take the mind off stressful things in your life. Moreover, a change in the oxygenation level of the blood provides a suitable state to assess the triggers with PFC-dominant thinking. Physical exercise also changes brain chemistry (we will discuss that more in Chapter Five on how to look after your brain), creating a more balanced mood and greater levels of brain plasticity.

Oxytocin

The third group of activities require the secretion of a brain chemical called oxytocin. We naturally get oxytocin when we hold a young baby (especially if it is our own child), stroke pets, cuddle loved ones, and have an orgasm. The evolutionary point of oxytocin was to trigger nurturing behaviours to protect more vulnerable people and increase the survival of the species. That allowed our children to safely explore the world while still being protected by the caregivers. Oxytocin also motivated us to look after our loved ones, as cooperation and altruism increased the chances of survival. In turn, we received a warm glowing feeling of love, relaxation and a peaceful mind. In that state, our neocortex is fully replenished and gets a great supply of oxygen and glucose, enabling us to have the best mental abilities such as sound decision-making, troubleshooting, creativity, learning, understanding other people's way of being and feeling compassion and empathy. So being in nurturing relationships with people we love can help to naturally regulate our emotional state. If we don't have access to this, we can provide it to ourselves to some extent as well. Oxytocin can be triggered by self-nurturing behaviours such as taking a warm bath, having a massage and helping others. In fact, being there for other people can distract us from our internal amygdala triggers, giving our body and brain a chance to replenish.

Developing mental habits to break the cycle

The most common gratitude practice involves writing five things that you are grateful for every day before sleep. Studies have shown that people who engage in this task for two weeks show higher levels of happiness and less anxiety. Just try to sit down with a blank piece of paper and write down five things that come to mind. They can be general big picture statements (such as having good health, food, being able to read and write) or specific (my husband making me a nice breakfast this morning; having an interesting chat with my neighbour). The more you practise this exercise, the easier it gets to come up with items, creating a brain highway to feeling that state of gratitude. In addition to changing brain chemistry, gratitude practice enables us to feed the amygdala with more objective information. It will notice negative events in the world by itself, so there's no need to put in extra effort on that, but adding positive information will help the amygdala to have a more balanced view. Very similarly, positive affirmations, developed first by Louise Hay (1984), can naturally soothe the amygdala. For them to be effective, they need to be specific and realistic, as the brain is not fooled easily. Effective positive affirmations could include some of the items on your gratitude list and encouraging messages communicated in a loving and caring way. Here are some examples:

- You are strong, healthy and safe; you are just beginning to discover your true potential.
- Your heart is beating every second, taking care of your body, and making sure that each cell in your body is well replenished and healthy.

Cognitive retraining of emotional patterns

Given that the emotional (amygdala) and rational (PFC) parts of the brain are connected, we can examine, challenge and change our emotional patterns with rational questioning. The most common approach in psychology for that is called cognitive appraisal. Cognitive appraisal consists of recognising what are you feeling, guessing what thoughts might have caused that feeling and challenging the thinking patterns in the hope of changing emotions. It has been used widely in the format of cognitive behavioural therapy (CBT). One model based on this, created by Albert Ellis (1991), is called ABC(DE). We experience a certain situation (activating event/adversity or A) individually based on our beliefs (B), which triggers certain emotional patterns (emotional consequences or C). These patterns are subconscious and based on amygdala-dominant thinking which distorts our understanding of reality, magnifies the amount of negativity and ignores positivity in our environment. When we bring awareness to these beliefs, then we can challenge and dispute them (D), which can change our thinking to PFC-dominant, which is much more objective and balanced (effective new beliefs or E), leading to a change in our emotional state.

Dr John Demartini (2013) suggests that often when we feel hard done by, sad or angry about a situation, it comes from seeing only half the picture. For instance, have you experienced the devastating break-up of a romantic relationship? In the moment when it ended, you were probably acutely aware of the downsides of the relationship ending (such as missing the person and the good times you had together) and your attention would have been mainly focused on the positive memories, ignoring the ones that weren't that great. That, needless to say, will have created despair. Dr Demartini invites us to balance the picture by focusing our attention on the things that were not working well in the relationship (all the bad memories you can muster) and all the upsides of the relationship ending. Make a list as long as you can think of, mentioning only the negative aspects of that relationship and all the positive sides of that relationship ending. The list could look like this:

- I often felt invisible to him.
- He was very smelly and made a huge mess in the house.

- I was so in love with him that I neglected to spend time with my friends.
- Our time together was taking time away from my hobbies.
- Focusing on him and being upset by things he said would ruin my productivity for days.
- I didn't sleep well and often woke up tired and in a bad mood.
- I didn't like the food he cooked and I was putting on weight from it.
- I was starting to compromise on what things I liked to do – for example, we only went to see movies he was interested in and never to a musical or jazz concert.
- He didn't want to have kids, so if I stayed with him I would never be able to have children.
- I didn't like his friends.

Now continue that list until you have about 50 items to give your brain enough evidence for a more balanced perspective. To come up with such a long list, you can use the technique from the previous chapter, going through each of the eight areas of your life and finding out how that relationship negatively influenced each of them. This method is not intended for you to just see the positives of a break-up everywhere – that would be ridiculous and delusional. What this method does, though, is create a more balanced perspective. Your amygdala will be naturally aware of all the downsides of the situation – we have to acknowledge that it sucks when a relationship comes to an end, there is no doubt about it – but we should not allow the amygdala to get carried away with distorted thinking otherwise any setback will create a major catastrophe. In directing the spotlight away from the negative aspects of the situation using the PFC, we allow ourselves to look at the benefits of the new situation and the drawbacks if the break-up didn't happen. That just balances out amygdala-dominant thinking and creates a more objective perspective on the situation. However, this activity doesn't come easily and we need to actively put effort in to do it. The amygdala is a selfish b*tch/bastard and wants to run the show, so it's easy to dwell in the puddle of sorrow – that's natural for our mammal brains – but we have the option of utilising our supercomputer – the PFC – to balance that out and create much more flexible thinking. As with any habit, it requires effort and practice.

You will rewire your emotional networks if you challenge your thinking on a daily basis just by asking yourself a few simple questions:

- Awareness of the trigger: What is one thing that is truly annoying me today?
- Honouring your amygdala's thinking: What is the one main negative of the situation? What is wrong with that situation?
- Engaging your PFC to balance your amygdala's thinking: What are the positives of the situation?

The more you practise it, the more it becomes second nature to create more and more flexible thinking.

Summary of Chapter Two

In this chapter, we discussed how emotions are a crucial way for our mammal brain to communicate quickly and crudely which situations are suitable for us and which ones might cause us harm. The mammal brain (especially the amygdala) is tuned to mainly notice dangers to keep us safe. However, it does not understand our modern way of life well and often creates danger signals when there is no real danger. Thus, we need to soothe the amygdala with activities such as slow breathing, time in nature, time with friends, exercise and other constructive hobbies that change our state of mind. In addition, we need to educate the amygdala using our prefrontal cortex about how things really work to create a more balanced perspective. Emotions also change the way our bodies function and the opposite is true as well – our bodily states can change our emotional states – so it is important to notice these patterns and adjust habits if needed. So if you are feeling anxious, check how many cups of coffee you have drunk and whether you have had proper nutritious food today. We will discuss the body–brain connection and how to look after your brain in Chapter Four. In the next chapter, we look at how our personalities and mindsets affect our emotional and behavioural patterns and address the big question – can we change who we are?

But before we move on, let's summarise what steps we need to go through to change our emotional patterns:

1. Acknowledge that *all* emotions have a purpose – they have developed to keep us safe, and steer us to the environment that is most suitable for us.
2. Emotional centres of the brain function in a subconscious manner. They are not rational. Thus, we cannot truly understand our emotions; we can just guess why we feel what we feel (rationalizing). Our rational minds cannot access the vastness of information accessible to the sub-conscious centres.
3. To ensure our survival, we need complex interaction between multiple brain systems such as the amygdala (threat detector), reward centres (pleasure detector), hypothalamus (brain–body connector), insula (body–brain connector), sympathetic nervous system (activator), parasympathetic nervous system (soother) and PFC (learner). They are all involved in creating and regulating our emotions and

influence our mental state and the behaviour we engage in under these emotions.

4. The amygdala keeps constantly searching for potential dangers to keep us safe. That's the job of this brain structure. However, it can severely distort our way of thinking, boosting all of the negativity in the world and ignoring all the positive and neutral experiences and memories. Also, the amygdala can easily get overwhelmed and in such a state can 'block' rational thinking (amygdala hijack of the rational brain). In that state, we cannot be sensible, so we just need to wait it out and not make *any* decisions for at least 15–30 minutes. To keep the amygdala in check, we need to do amygdala-soothing activities, such as breathing exercises, meditation, and time in nature, on a daily basis.

5. The PFC is the most sensible part of our brains and can provide a reality check to the amygdala once it is calm enough (it needs to be calmed down with amygdala-soothing techniques first if it is raging). PFC-driven approaches include the ABC(DE) model from cognitive behavioural therapy, and various coaching techniques, like the ones designed by Dr John Demartini (2013) I have discussed in this chapter.

CHAPTER THREE

Changing Your Personality

In this chapter, you will learn:

- Whether we are born with our personality or whether we can change it.
- What perception bias is and why you should care.
- How to find out what our true values are and how they influence our lives.
- Fixed and growth mindsets and how they influence our ability to change.
- Practical steps on how to promote a growth mindset and change unwanted personality traits.

Why do we sometimes struggle to understand other people? One of the main reasons is that each of us has a very biased representation of the world in our brains. We never perceive the world exactly as it is. Our brains are very selective and notice only those things we have previously labelled as important. Moreover, we can only remember a very small part of what we notice for a short time – in the long term, we remember even less.

Based on this limited information, we form our model of the world, which directs our actions and attitudes and forms the basis of our personality traits. To make matters worse, what we notice becomes a self-fulfilling prophecy – the decisions and observations we have made further bias our perception process, making us more likely to notice facts that support our past observations. This is called attention bias – or, to use a more scientific term, top-down modulation of the brain area called *the thalamus*. As a result, we get stuck in our ways, making spontaneous change nearly impossible.

So what is the answer if we do want to change? First of all, if we want to truly change, we need to challenge our existing model of the world. Our intrinsic mental maps are filled with assumptions of what it is like to be a successful person, what good relationships look like, how we deal with failure, and so on. We learn most of these ideas during childhood, based on what we have been exposed to, and some later in life, but either way most of them are hidden in our unconscious mind and we are not really aware of them. Thus, the first step is to bring these assumptions into the conscious mind and challenge them – some of them will still be correct, while others will seem ridiculous so we will need to replace them with more accurate insights. In doing so, we can update our intrinsic model of who we are and bit by bit create a change in our behaviour and personality.

This process can be influenced, though, by our attitudes, or mindset, as described by Carol Dweck (2017): if we think that our character traits are inherent (fixed mindset), we will not do the work needed to challenge and change them. The good news is that neuroscience has provided a vast amount of evidence that our brains can change throughout life, supporting the idea of the growth mindset. So in this chapter, we also look at why we sometimes get 'stuck' in a fixed mindset, how that affects our brain plasticity and how to get our brains 'unstuck' and promote a growth mindset, which is crucial in changing personality traits, attitudes and behaviour.

Identical twin experiments suggest that 50 per cent of our personality traits are determined by our genes (so you always have a reason to blame your parents!), 15 per cent are defined by environmental factors (in particular, what we have been exposed to in the womb and early childhood, again – blame your parents!), and 35 per cent are determined by the choices we make. Here, you can try to blame somebody else, such as that nasty teacher or the girlfriend/boyfriend who dumped you, but ultimately you can do something about it. In this chapter, we will look at that 35 per cent – the way you perceive the world and how your values, choices and mindset affect the way you are and how you can change that.

Perception bias – we never see the world as it is!

The outer layer of your brain, called the neocortex, or what Paul MacLean (1990) calls the human brain in his Triune Brain model, consists of four large parts: the frontal lobes, the parietal lobes, the temporal lobes and the occipital lobes, which shape the way we perceive the world and interact with it.

The frontal lobes are positioned at the very front of your brain underneath your forehead. The largest part of these, the prefrontal cortex (PFC), produces rational thinking, willpower, allows us to control our emotions and is important for personality. If this area gets damaged through an injury or illness, patients often see their personality change and are unable to suppress their anger and frustration or to delay gratification. Behind the PFC is the motor cortex, which enables us to write, drive, kick a ball and do other physical tasks. Right underneath it is Broca's area of speech, which is crucial for verbalising your thoughts.

The parietal lobes are positioned at the top of your head after the motor cortex. The somatosensory cortex part of these lobes receives sensations from your skin such as temperature, touch and pain, allowing you to quickly realise if your tea is too hot to drink, to enjoy a nice cuddle from a special friend and to know if your shoes are much too uncomfortable to wear. The parietal lobes are also crucial for understanding symbols, such as letters and numbers, allowing you to read this page. Moreover, this area allows some of us to park a car without scratching the alloy wheels. This skill is called spatial awareness, which sadly I am not blessed with.

Moving towards the sides of your head, just underneath your temples are *the temporal lobes*, which receive information from your ears, thus part of this area is called the auditory cortex. It enables you to appreciate music, hear the hooting of a car and, perhaps most importantly, make sense of human language. The area that is important for language comprehension is called Wernicke's area and, if damaged, it makes it really hard to both understand others and also to express ourselves in a way that makes sense.

At the very back of the brain are *the occipital lobes*, which receive information from your eyes and are responsible for vision and making sense of objects you see. This area is also called the visual cortex and, if damaged, can result in vision impairments.

Needless to say, all of these brain areas work in a coordinated manner when we do almost anything. Imagine yourself driving a car or riding a bicycle. Your frontal lobes plan the route and help you focus only on essential information so you don't get distracted. Your parietal lobes allow you to have a sense of your positioning in regard to other objects on the road. The somatosensory cortex of the parietal lobes gives you the sensation of holding a steering wheel, while your motor cortex of the frontal lobes enables you to steer it. Your visual cortex enables you to predict the speed and direction of other vehicles. In the meantime, the auditory cortex enables you to hear the directions your satnav is giving you and also to quickly react if there is an ambulance siren coming your way.

Figuring out important information

In order to gain a better understanding of how our brains decide what information is important, we have to look at the brain structure deep in the centre of the brain called the thalamus.

The thalamus receives signals from sensory systems (other than smell), such as the eyes, ears, taste buds on the tongue, and skin, and sends the information to the relevant centres of the brain. Let's take the part of the thalamus that is responsible for vision, called the lateral geniculate nucleus (LGN). The LGN receives visual information from your eyes and has to send it to the part of the visual cortex called V1. However, V1 can also moderate the activity of the LGN via the so-called thalamocortical loop, making it more or less sensitive to certain visual cues (this is also called top-down modulation or internally driven attention). In other words, the visual cortex tells the thalamus which objects to search for and which to ignore, making our visual perception biased. If you are driving a car, your visual cortex will 'tell' your thalamus that other cars, the road and traffic lights are important objects, so it will make sure that you notice everything related to those. The visual cortex can also 'tell' the thalamus that pedestrians on the pavement, shop windows and what other drivers look like are irrelevant distractions, so the thalamus will filter those out.

This thalamocortical loop also filters the way we perceive the world based on our inner beliefs. Let's say you go outside and walk along the street with the belief that everyone in your city is miserable. Needless to say, you will find plenty of examples where that holds true. Now imagine you give your thalamus a different 'task' – go out and try to find the opposite, search for people who display happiness, and you might be able to find quite a few. Of course, both are true – there are plenty of unhappy people on your streets at this very moment, but there are also a lot of happy ones. However, if you remember from the previous chapter, the amygdala will be biasing your beliefs to avoid danger so it will make sure that you notice and remember everything that is negative. For that very reason, many of us become more and more pessimistic over time – 'search and you shall find' your brain would say.

Individual value hierarchy

Our past experiences and expectations bias the way we perceive the world, but there is one more crucial factor creating a filter for what we notice, remember and take action on: our individual values. Let's walk through a busy shopping mall together. Somebody like my cousin Beatrice, who values fashion, will notice beauty products, fashionable bags and trendy shoes. A person like me, who has young children or is desperate to have some, will notice buggies, toys and baby clothes (oh they are so cute!). A person who is into rock climbing and outdoors pursuits, like my husband Matthew, will pay attention to all the climbing shoes and mountaineering equipment. Imagine now that we are each given £500. I would immediately buy my daughter Emilija a bouncy castle for our garden. Beatrice would probably buy make-up, a pair of trendy jeans and, of course, stylish shoes. Matthew, however, will choose a very light tent for his Alpine adventures or a pair of skiing boots. So which one of us is right and which of us has wasted our money? I hope you understand that it's a ridiculous question. Each of us has a unique set of values, which makes us who we are. For the things that are high on our individual value list, we are always motivated, resourceful, attentive and creative. We naturally become good at the things we value as we spend so much time focusing on them and practising them. However, we lack motivation for the things that are at the bottom of our value list. We easily procrastinate, have issues paying attention (try to watch a political debate with me) and very easily forget key information. Therefore, truly understanding who you are and how to be an effective human being requires first understanding your current individual value hierarchy and then linking your activities and planning your professional and personal life according to it.

The value determination process

According to Dr John Demartini (2013), in order to understand what we truly value, we need to examine the life we live and the things we naturally do. His method includes 13 simple questions to examine your current life as honestly as possible.

1. How do you fill your personal space? What are the top three things that surround your working room, living room, bedroom, car or any other space?

2. How do you spend your time? What are the top three activities that you always find time for?

3. How do you spend your energy? What are the top three things you always have the energy for?

4. How do you spend your money? What are the top three things that you always find the money for?

5. Where do you have the most order and organisation? What are the top three things that you are really organised with? Think about anything in your life, be it physical (objects) or more abstract (meetings with people, ideas, music and so on).

6. Where are you most reliable, disciplined and focused? What are the top three areas in your life that you always show up for with clear mental focus?

7. What do you think about, and what is your most dominant thought? What are the top three topics that are always on your mind? In this part, it is sometimes tricky to separate amygdala-dominant negative mind chatter from value-driven thoughts, but just write down the areas that these thoughts represent to you (so if you are constantly thinking 'Am I a good enough mother?', the area would be motherhood or children, while 'Will I lose my job?' thoughts could represent career or financial safety – choose whichever feels more accurate).

8. What do you visualise and realise? What are the top three areas in your life that you have dreamed about and slowly but surely made your visions come true?

9. What is your internal dialogue? What are the top three things you internally debate about? This is pretty similar to most dominant thoughts; again, write about which internal conversations represent you.

10. What do you talk about in social settings? What are the top three topics you always fall into in your conversations with others?

11. What inspires you? What are the top three topics or kinds of people that inspire you most?

12. What are the most consistent long-term goals that you have set? What are the top three plans/dreams/goals that you have had in your mind for a long time?

13. What do you love to learn and read about most? What are the top three topics that you are always drawn to while browsing in bookshops and on the internet or love attending talks or seminars about?

Now that we have completed these 13 questions, we need to go through the answers and count how many times we have repeated the same answers or group them in the categories of similar answers. My top three values are: my daughter Emilija, my work (university lectures, public seminars, coaching clients, writing this book) and my relationship with my husband, each scoring the same (13 points). These values do change, of course, in different stages in life. I used to place a much higher value on cycling, climbing and time with friends. Since Emilija was born I barely cycle, climb only every now and then and have recreated a friends group with other parents – and that feels good for me. However, there is something that can cloud your value hierarchy: forcing your old values or other people's values into your value list. So, another aspect of truly being who you are is to examine whether your life is congruent with your true values or if you have incorporated other people's priorities into your list. If you try to live by other people's values, it will have a negative effect on your productivity, reliability and, most noticeably, motivation. Inevitably, you will also feel lost. In the next section, we will look at how to resolve that.

Letting go of other people's values

Each of us has a unique value hierarchy, which guides us to do what feels meaningful. However, we often assimilate the values of authority figures (parents, teachers, people we are infatuated with) or the norms of society, and that can inevitably create inner conflict. If your mind is full of 'shoulds' you never act on, then write them all down. Think of as many of them as you can and put them all down on paper. My list might look something like this:

1. I should be stricter with Emilija and get her into a better routine.
2. I should ask Matthew to do 50/50 parenting.
3. I should exercise more and get back to being a strong cyclist.
4. I should do really hard-core research and aim to start my own research team one day.
5. I should call my friends more.

I could continue with this list, but let's stop here and challenge them. Whose voices are really speaking here? Actually, each of them stems from different people: 1) Other parents from my NCT (National Childbirth Trust) group whose kids were in a 7 p.m. to 7 a.m. sleeping routine from early on. 2) The feminist movement but especially some of my friends who are very much pro 50/50 parenting. 3) That's myself from 2013, when cycling was a big deal for me. I still have my racing bike from that time and get that little voice in my mind whenever I see it. 4) That was my ambition at the start of my PhD, but doesn't apply to me in the same sense at this stage in life. 5) In fact, this is my friends talking. Friendship is a very high priority for them, as it was for me in the past when I was single and chose to spend a lot more time socialising than I do now.

If we want to go even further, we can ask another question: what would be the drawbacks of me doing these things? 1) Emilija wouldn't get to see Matthew in the evenings as he works late and, also, I wouldn't be able to work in the mornings, which I really enjoy. I love having time in the mornings for myself and usually do my best writing then. 2) Well, Matthew does work 10–12-hour days in his chiropractic practice, making sure all of his patients are well taken care of. He manages to get a lot of people from agony to a pain-free state and it feels so important to him and consequently to me that he does that rather than playing with Emilija. Also, I love my time with Emilija! She is so funny and I love teaching her to talk, dancing, reading books, cooking, going for walks with her. If I am honest, I don't want to reduce the time I spend doing that. 3) Getting back into cycling in the way I used to would mean that I wouldn't have as much time to work on this book, read research papers, create lectures and seminars, play with Emilija or spend time with Matthew. I wouldn't change any of them for cycling. 4) Currently I lecture at a university, give seminars in companies, coach clients and work on this book. I love my work, which unfortunately I didn't during my PhD when I was involved in cutting-edge experiments, but then those weren't linked to my highest value – helping people by sharing knowledge. 5) Spending more time talking to friends would take time away from writing, reading and playing with Emilija. It would feel forced if I tried to call them more than I want to and would probably backfire by creating resentment.

Challenging 'shoulds' is a process and might need revisiting a few times, but overall, writing them down, understanding where they come from and assessing them will do the job. The next thing to address is mindset – a set of beliefs about what is and what isn't possible to change in our personality traits, talents and capabilities.

Fixed and growth mindsets

In order to change our habits, personality traits or emotional patterns, we must first believe that this change is possible otherwise we won't even bother to put in the work and effort needed to change these brain networks. However, most of us sometimes slip into the belief that we just are the way we are and we can't really change. That attitude researcher Carol Dweck (2017) has called a *fixed mindset*. In the fixed mindset, we think intelligence, talent and character traits are predetermined and there is not much we can do about them. As a result, we avoid new challenges and take on tasks that we know we can manage. That approach just strengthens the existing neural pathways, making us more set in our ways and robbing our brains of opportunities to create new pathways and learn new skills. Not surprisingly, that approach reduces brain plasticity. Interestingly, brain plasticity adapts to our lifestyle – it increases when it's needed (when we travel, build new relationships, exercise or learn new skills) and reduces when we are not using it (stuck in the same habits, isolating ourselves, leading sedentary lifestyles) or when body and brain think that we are in survival mode, which is determined by high levels of cortisol in the blood.

In contrast, when we are in a so-called *growth mindset* (Dweck, 2017), we are much more open-minded – we believe that certain aspects of intelligence, talent and personality can be changed. As a result, we try new things, put more effort into the skills we are not that great at (yet) and challenge our character traits. Needless to say, that increases brain plasticity and the chance of changing these traits becomes higher. Both mindsets have a different effect on our brain states and behaviour. In a fixed mindset, we make our behaviour less varied and reduce brain plasticity, making it almost impossible to change. In contrast, a growth mindset widens our repertoire of activities and increases brain plasticity, making it much more possible to create a lasting change. So in that way, mindsets create a self-fulfilling prophecy. Moreover, whether we are in a fixed or growth mindset affects the way we deal with challenges.

In a fixed mindset, we take any success as proof that we are superior and failure as evidence of our inherent flaws. Not surprisingly, with these beliefs we get very cocky when things go well, and will hide our failures or find external causes to blame for them. When we do not achieve the results we intended to, a fixed mindset creates an amygdala-dominant reaction to it, steering us away from trying again. A fixed mindset pushes us to quit easily. Believing that there is not much we can do to get better, we try to put others down or invalidate their success by attributing it to external factors. We become competitive, secretive and, let's be honest, not that fun to be around. A fixed mindset takes a big toll on our emotional wellbeing as it constantly triggers the amygdala, which in turn compromises the functioning of the PFC. Reduced activity of the PFC creates less flexibility in thinking, keeping us stuck in a fixed mindset. It's a bit of a downward spiral.

In contrast, in the state of the growth mindset, we believe that achieving results depends on many factors, hard work and perseverance being at the core of it. If we encounter setbacks, we either work harder or adjust our approach slightly and try again. In this state, we are flexible, adaptable and open-minded. In a fixed mindset, we take feedback as criticism and we either invalidate it ('she just doesn't like me' or 'that might have worked for them, but it won't work for me') or challenge it. In a growth mindset, we are capable of listening to feedback without our PFC being hijacked by the amygdala, thus, we can assess the feedback, take what works from it or challenge it in an adult manner ('thank you for this information, I can see how it could work; however, it doesn't meet these criteria').

Let's take Monica and Dominic. They are both senior executives in the same company but they have very different ways of thinking about themselves and others. If you ask Monica how she got to this stage of her career, she will tell you that she had a passion for industry, was determined and worked very hard for it. Dominic will tell you that he was always very smart, in fact the smartest in the class, and as a result he didn't need to work hard to get to where he is. He attributes his success to inherent qualities of intellect – admitting to hard work would challenge his superior intelligence. Although Monica has a higher IQ score than Dominic and was always a top student, she somehow doesn't see that as a big deal. She attributes her achievements to a combination of factors such as a desire to do a good job, the ability to learn, dedication and responsibility.

When asked about their hobbies, Dominic shares that he does Thai boxing, something he has a natural aptitude for. He has tried a few other things – racing car driving, rock climbing and playing the guitar, but gave up on each of these activities within a month, as it was clear that he was *never* going to be good at them. Monica is currently really into CrossFit but she has had a number of hobbies over the years: she has been training and competed in amateur track cycling, learned to play the piano to a pretty decent standard and has a passion for learning foreign languages by living abroad for one month each summer (she is really good at Italian now and talks to me in my native Lithuanian language pretty well too!). Monica doesn't care too much if she is good at an activity; she follows her passion and interests and then puts the work and dedication into them. As a result, she is now good at a wide range of things. By contrast, Dominic doesn't speak any foreign languages ('I am just not gifted at that') or play a music instrument ('My parents didn't take me to music school during my childhood. Also, nobody in my family plays a musical instrument'). As you can see, both fixed and growth mindsets create a self-fulfilling prophecy, thus, they become a key aspect of our personalities. The key question then is 'Can we change our mindset?'

Steps to cultivating a growth mindset

In order to address changing the mindset, let's first take a look at how mindset develops. Imagine Dominic's parents. Success was always very important to them, thus, noticing that he was a sharp boy, they couldn't stop praising him for that: 'You are so clever!', 'You are really talented', 'This boy will go far'. That didn't stop at intellect, as he was praised for his looks: 'What beautiful brown eyes and a perfect body type' and character traits: 'He is just a natural leader, he won't take commands from anyone'. All of these compliments addressed the qualities he had no control over (at least not in the way a child's mind can perceive these statements), therefore these statements created fixed ideas of who he is and is not. At school, Dominic found a way to assert himself as being smart, always in the right, and he wasn't open to feedback from his teachers or peers. In fact, most teachers, according to him, were just stupid, and that's why he sometimes didn't get the highest grade. The ones who praised his intellect though were good teachers, of course. These praising statements from parents, although well meant, ingrain deep-rooted beliefs in the young child's brain about the permanence of the qualities they possess (you either are intelligent/talented at sports/good-looking, and so on, or you are not).

Now let's look at Monica's upbringing. Her start in life was similar – she was a smart, athletic and beautiful child. However, Monica's parents did not treat her in a special way because of this. If she came back from school with an A in maths, she got praised for the work she put in to understand all the equations. When Monica got an award for the best essay of the year, her dad was really proud of how much work and dedication she put into expressing her imaginative thoughts in words. If Monica took time to match her clothes well and do her hair, grandma would praise her for the efforts she put into creating such a stylish look. Although Monica got plenty of praise in her childhood, it was all directed at something she had control over – how much time she spent doing maths homework, how much effort she put into writing (and rewriting) her essay, how much thought she gave to matching her outfit. In secondary school, Monica made friends with Liz, who was a school champion in tennis. Monica was fascinated by how quickly Liz could move on the tennis court and became determined to learn. Every day after lessons, Monica would watch Liz training on the tennis court and she started having lessons with the coach. Slowly but surely, she learned to play fairly well and was quick to adjust if she got any feedback from Liz. Over two years, Monica got so good that she could play a very close game with Liz and even won a number of times against her. Now what would Dominic have done in the same situation? As you can probably guess, he would have taken his inability to play tennis as an almost inherent quality (remember, when we get into a fixed mindset, our thinking becomes binary – you are either good at it or not, with no space in between). If encouraged, he might have tried once or twice and, seeing that Liz was just so much better than him, he would have probably given up, concluding that it was just not his sport. So how could Dominic bridge the gap between a fixed mindset and a growth mindset?

First, we need to help Dominic to challenge his thinking with questions that provoke PFC-dominant thinking. One technique I find tremendously useful with my coaching clients is from The Work method by Byron Katie (Katie & Mitchell, 2002). This technique consists of six questions that take you through the process of revaluation and rediscovery. Let's take one statement Dominic might be sure of: 'I am just no good at tennis', and let's challenge it through the six stages of The Work method:

1. Me: Is that true?

Dominic: Yes.

2. Me: Dominic, can you be absolutely sure that you are no good at tennis?

Dominic: Well, I can't be absolutely sure, of course, as I haven't really played it much.

3. Me: When you believe that you are no good at tennis, how does it make you feel and what is it that you do?

Dominic: Well, I feel like a loser and I don't want to do it. I also get angry when I see people play it and think that they are stupid for enjoying it and don't want to hang around them. So I go home and watch TV.

4. Me: OK, now imagine for a moment that you could no longer think the thought that you are no good at tennis; how would that feel and what would you do?

Dominic (after a little hesitation): I would not be upset about it; I would just try it for a while and see if I enjoyed it. If I did, I would continue to play for fun and might make some new friends while doing so. If I really enjoyed it, I might play often and perhaps get really good at it with practice. If I didn't enjoy it, then I wouldn't bother with it, but at least I would know that I had given it a go. I feel like I am giving up on something I don't even know, so at least then I would know if it's my thing or not. I would also be less judgemental about people who enjoy it (and are good at it).

5. Me: So do you see any reasons for you to give up the thought that you are not good at tennis?

Dominic: Well, sort of. I can see that it would be a lot less stressful for me and others, perhaps.

6. Me: Would you like for us now to try to come up with any other thoughts that would feel as true or truer than the initial belief?

Dominic: Sure (a bit sceptically).

Me: We will change just one word in the sentence at a time. So let's take the initial belief 'I am just no good at tennis' and change it to the opposite.

Dominic: I am just good at tennis?

Me: That's right. Could this be as true as the initial statement?

Dominic: Ah, I see where you are going! Since I haven't really tried it, it could be as true or truer. I won't know until I actually give it a proper go.

Me: That's right. Let's try another one. Take the initial belief and change it to the other.

Dominic: Somebody else is just not good at tennis?

Me: Sure, think about it. Do you know anyone else who you really like and perhaps admire, who is no good at tennis?

Dominic (laughing): I do actually – my girlfriend Joanna. She is awesome, but really looks so funny when she plays tennis. I actually really love that she is still trying and I am sure she will get good at it with her brilliant mind and strong legs. Oh wow, that's really strange. I have been talking about the same thing – the inability to play tennis – in such different ways when it is myself or when it is Joanna. Wow, crazy.

Me: Interesting, isn't it? Shall we try one more turnaround? (Dominic nods his head). This one is trickier, but let's try – let's swap 'I' and 'tennis'.

Dominic: Tennis is just not good at me?

Me: That's right. Let's sit with it and see if any interpretation of this statement could make any sense.

Dominic: I am not sure if that would work, but the first thought that comes to my mind is that I am frustrated by and resentful of tennis as a whole. When I am not good at it, it's almost like it's pointing out my shortcomings.

Me: That's good! Keep going.

Dominic: Well, it's just that I enjoy being good at things and hate it being pointed out that there are some things I am not good at. So it's almost like tennis is a person with a finger pointing at my flaws and saying, 'You are not that great after all'. Does that sound crazy?

Me: No, no, that's great, it's good crazy. Crazy helps us expand our thinking, doesn't it?

Dominic: Definitely! I can see now how silly of me it was to put so much importance and stress on something that I haven't even properly given a go yet.

Me: So which belief related to tennis would you like to keep?

Dominic: I don't know yet if I am any good at tennis or not, but I might give it a go, perhaps with Joanna when she is free next. Can't wait actually, it will be fun.

In this process I just asked Dominic questions to challenge his thinking. I didn't point out the mistakes in his thinking but was just being curious and he did all the work himself – acknowledged the logical flaws in his thinking, assessed the effects his thinking was having on him, and came up with alternatives. He was able to step up to the situation with a much more PFC-dominant attitude. It shows that when the amygdala is calm, the PFC will do the rest.

When trying to foster a growth mindset in people (including ourselves) it is also important to be thoughtful about how we give the feedback – am I focusing on something the person can change?

Summary of Chapter Three

To summarise, our genes determine 50 per cent of our personality traits, our upbringing influences another 15 per cent, but there is still 35 per cent we can change to some extent.

However, in order to create that change we need to go through the following steps:

1. Realise that our brains are biased and the way we perceive the world is never objective. If we have certain observations that are getting in the way of achieving what is important to us, we can challenge that perception and search for the opposite.
2. Understand our true value hierarchy, which determines further what things we notice and which areas of life we flourish in.
3. Declutter our 'shoulds' – they just get in the way of us embracing what things we truly want to do and might lead us further away from the professional and personal life circumstances that truly work for us.
4. Challenge the times when we get into a fixed mindset – it's very much amygdala-dominant thinking that wants to keep us safe, but, unfortunately, keeps us stuck in the old behaviour patterns.
5. Cultivate a growth mindset by challenging fixed mindset beliefs and changing our focus to the things we can actually control.

PART II

Changing the Results

CHAPTER FOUR

Changing Your Productivity

In this chapter, you will learn:

- What is needed for our brains to be productive at work.
- How we form memories, why our memory gets worse over time and whether we can improve it. (We can!)
- What happens in the brain when we multitask.
- Why our attention span is getting shorter and whether we can increase it.
- All about the magical power of of motivation and practical tools to boost it.
- Why we procrastinate more and more over time and what is needed for us to stop it.

Your brain is constantly changing. Did you have a much better memory as a child? Were you able to concentrate on reading a book for a long period of time whereas now you can barely finish a full article on the internet? Do you tend to procrastinate and feel unable to stop, no matter how hard you try? Were you once a much more optimistic person, but now struggle to feel happy about your life?

These are just a few examples of how your brain is constantly changing based on what you do most often (it's activity-dependent brain plasticity again). If you would like to take charge of how your brain develops then this chapter is exactly what you need: first, to understand the mechanisms underlying high performance, memory formation, attention and productivity, and second, to successfully train your brain to be better at tasks once again.

Empowering the prefrontal cortex

The prefrontal cortex (PFC) enables us to control our emotions and have willpower, focused attention, working memory and motivation. Thus, for us to perform well, the PFC needs to be replenished. As we have already discussed in Chapter One, this brain region contains very large neural networks and needs enormous amounts of energy. If we are short of energy due to lack of nutrients, lack of rest, or insufficient replenishment, we revert to more automatic behaviours and ways of thinking governed by older mammal brain regions. So, let's look at what habits enable the PFC to function at its best.

First, we need to make sure that the PFC neurons get enough nutrients and oxygen. We can do this by eating regular, nutritious meals, making sure our breathing is slow and deep (or at least remembering every now and then to come back to slow breathing) and doing regular exercise to increase blood oxygenation levels and expand our blood vessels.

Second, we need to alternate times of work and rest. During activity, neurons release chemicals called neurotransmitters, which enable them to communicate with other neurons. These chemicals then need to be taken away from the gap between the neurons, called the synapse, and recycled or got rid of, which requires action from separate types of cells called glia cells. If we use the same neurons for an extended period of time, they deplete the neurotransmitters, and subsequently cannot function as well. Also, the overload of neurotransmitters that needs to be processed by the glia cells increases the risk of so-called activity-induced neurotoxicity, which further compromises the activity of these neurons. Thus, the solution is simple – we need to take breaks. I am often asked how frequent the breaks should be, but the answer is not easy. The number of breaks required depends on the complexity of the task, your individual brain activity and, perhaps most importantly, what emotions this activity causes for you. So the frequency and the duration of breaks needs to be tailored to your individual case. If in doubt though, I would suggest starting with taking a ten-minute break every hour-and-a-half in the mornings and increasing the frequency to ten minutes every hour after lunch. It sounds like a lot to some, but if we monitor the amount of time we spend in unstructured browsing when experiencing mental fatigue, that will suddenly seem not so much. It also creates more structure for work and a clear separation between work and rest, which is beneficial for attention training, which I will elaborate on later.

Third, we have to make sure we get enough sleep. When we sleep, the PFC neurons are resting and they are replenishing their neurotransmitter storage which will be required another day. Moreover, the glia cells in the PFC and other regions clear the damage done to the networks due to neural activity (the activity-dependent neurotoxicity already mentioned). Sleep is crucial for neural maturation – the new neurons that are born in the region called the dentate gyrus get incorporated into the neural networks, enabling life-long learning, the acquisition of new skills, and agility in thinking. If that wasn't enough to make you take your sleep seriously, sleep is crucial for memory as the information we learn during the day gets converted into a long-term memory by the brain region called the hippocampus when we sleep (a process called memory consolidation).

Last but not least, if we use physical exercise as our means to relax, it not only increases oxygenation of the blood and dilates blood vessels, enabling neurons to be well nourished, but it also increases brain plasticity. Experiments with rats who were doing the exercise they enjoyed (you know rats – running in mazes and on treadmills) showed increased levels of brain-derived neurotropic factor (BDNF) in comparison to the ones who were lazy. Interestingly, the ones who were forced to exercise in ways they didn't enjoy didn't increase their BDNF, meaning that only voluntary enjoyable physical activity improves brain plasticity. BDNF is required for the formation of new networks, which is crucial for learning, mental agility and the ability to change habits.

In terms of creating time for these replenishment stages, some of you might need to become more efficient with your time first. The more efficient we get with basic tasks, the more time we have to replenish our PFC to optimise it for further use. So here is a suggestion that might be helpful. You might want to start with an inventory of existing habits: write down everything you do in a day (or ideally in a week). Then look at which tasks could be grouped together, in what is called batch processing – for example, multiple grocery shops could be grouped together and perhaps, even better, you could create an automated weekly grocery order you don't need to worry about. Check which tasks on your list could be delegated to somebody else or automated. Ask yourself: which of these tasks could you do without? If you struggle with constant mental fatigue, one thing is for sure – the number of tasks you do during the day needs to be trimmed to the most important ones. It's crucial to be as honest with yourself as possible about what could be taken off the list. Also, how many tasks do you normally put on your to-do list? The more tasks you have there, the more distracting it is for your PFC, wasting its resources and creating a bigger sense of urgency and stress. I suggest starting your day with this question: What is the most important thing for me to do today? If you can, start with that task first thing and when you complete that, ask yourself the following: What is the second most important thing for me to do today? As you can see, this creates sequential rather than parallel processing of priorities, which is much less distracting to the PFC and creates fewer chances for procrastination to be triggered.

Improving memory

Let's look now at what is needed for us to convert information into a long-term memory. First, there are different kinds of memory, each of them encoded by different brain areas. Information we store and can retrieve on demand (useful for quizzes) is called explicit or declarative memory.

Explicit memory consists of two types: *semantic*, or memory for facts such as remembering the capital cities of various countries, names of football players, or lines from the movies, and *episodic* memory, which enables us to recall the events of our lives or the lives of others (including movie or book plots and major events in society). These forms of memory are encoded by different parts of the brain, with the temporal lobes taking care of semantic memory, while the PFC, hippocampus and regions next to the hippocampus (the parahippocampal cortex) are crucial for episodic memory.

Implicit, also called non-declarative memory, consists of procedural memory, conditioning and priming. Procedural memory enables us to acquire skills, such as learning to drive a car or play a musical instrument, and develop habitual behaviour patterns, such as opening the fridge when you are hungry or navigating to work without even thinking about it. Basal ganglia, the cerebellum and parts of the motor cortex are crucial for automating these motoric kinds of learning. Conditioning can be divided into two kinds: cerebellum-governed classical conditioning, which makes us salivate when we hear the plates rattling in the kitchen, and amygdala-ruled emotional conditioning, which creates automatic emotional reactions to things like snakes, flights or triggers of past trauma. Priming can be illustrated by filling in the missing gaps in the text or the ability to read jumbled text such as this, based on our frequent past experience of reading these words in the correct form: It deosn't mttaer in waht oredr the ltteers in a wrod are, the olny iprmoatnt tihng is taht the frist and lsat ltteer are in the rghit pclae. The rset can be a toatl mses and you can sitll raed it wouthit porbelm. Tihs is bcuseae the huamn mnid deos not raed ervey lteter by istlef, but the wrod as a wlohe.

When I used to teach neuroscience in schools I would ask my pupils – which types of memory are you good at? At first this puzzled them – we are so used to valuing our capacity to remember based on explicit types of memory. However, other types are also crucial in our productivity and performance. So if you have a moment, reflect on and assess how good each type of your memory is – just self-assess how well you perform in each type and give it a score from 1 to 10. To take it further, you can also ask yourself how you use the different types of memory to aid your performance. Think about which type of memory you want to systematically train to be better. I am, for example, training my procedural memory by finding new opportunities to practise it – parking a car in small gaps, rock climbing, learning techniques for chiropractic adjustments from my husband, and I keep meaning to start learning the piano. My good episodic memory allows me to recall the movements my husband made when he was showing me how to adjust the lower back from a side posture or the actions my mother-in-law took when she parked her car perfectly in a very small gap.

Another aspect of memory is *attention*. We are constantly surrounded by varied sensory information: smells, sounds, touch and visual stimuli. However, we can only truly pay attention to a fraction of this. These inputs enter our sensory memory, which lasts for only a fraction of a second. But the senses we pay attention to enter the next stage – short-term memory – and all the unattended information is simply lost. Short-term memory, also called the working memory in the case of explicit memory types, holds information only long enough (15–30 seconds) for us to do something with it (like remembering somebody's phone number for long enough to enter it in your contacts). However, we can extend it by repetition (for example, repeating a phone number in your mind if you are trying to memorise it, or repeating the sounds of a foreign phrase) or multiple exposure (for example, listening to a song a number of times to remember the lyrics or reading a sentence a few times to capture the words). We can also increase our chances of remembering it long-term if we think about it in a more complex manner such as grouping, seeing patterns in numbers or creating a rhyme to it. Only the information we truly pay attention to, rehearse enough or attach meaning to enters the next stage – the long-term memory. The brain structure called the hippocampus is crucial for converting information from the short-term to the long-term memory, and, as I mentioned earlier, it mainly happens when we sleep or have downtime. For information to be stored in the neural networks – encoding these memories – it needs to change through physical changes in the connections (called the synapses) between neurons. This process is called long-term potentiation (LTP), and the more we repeat that information, the more LTP these synapses experience, making subsequent networks stronger and more robust. Over time, some information fades away – what we call forgetting – which is an important part of memory. The brain wants to store only things that are relevant and gets rid of facts that are not important, to allow space for new memories to be encoded. To fix gaps in memories, your brain fills in the missing information with plausible bits based on the context. If you have been to many birthday parties and might not remember what you ate at Julia's 18th, your brain might fill these missing gaps with memories from other birthdays, such as cake, sausage rolls and fruit. Also, spookily, we can implant false memories in others using convincing stories, especially if it's a period they can't remember very well, such as early childhood.

The more we repeat the information and the more closely we pay attention to it, the more robust brain networks we build and the more reliable memories we possess.

Next, we will look at different types of attention and some practical tools for how to train them.

Multitasking and training attention

A crucial component of sharp performance, productivity and good memory is the attention span. We cannot focus on more than four to seven items in our working memory (known as cognitive load), making it physically impossible for us to truly multitask. When we multitask, we keep on switching our attention from the task we have been doing to something else and then back to the task. This is called sequential processing. Although the switching is pretty fast – a fraction of a second – if we do that all the time, we can waste a staggering amount of time. The more tasks we keep on switching between, the more time we waste. For example, if we get 100 per cent of productivity when we focus on one task (let's say writing this chapter), we get 40 per cent of productive time per task when we focus on two projects (let's say we add making presentation slides for my upcoming seminar). Twenty per cent of the time gets wasted just by switching between these two. Let's not stop there – adding a third task, such as replying to emails, makes productivity just 20 per cent per task, and means that writing this chapter takes five times longer, and 40 per cent of time gets wasted in switching. We can go on, but the idea is simple: the more tasks you focus on, the more time you waste. Moreover, we are about three times more likely to make mistakes when we switch between even just two projects, and that applies for both letter-based (reading, writing, searching for typos) and numerical (accounting, doing home finance, helping your kids with maths homework) tasks.

Therefore, in order to perform well and be productive, we first need to train our attention span. In the brain, there are two different attention systems: the dorsal, also called top-down, attention system, which focuses on your internal thoughts, and the ventral, also called bottom-up, attention system, which makes sure we are in tune with what is happening around us. Needless to say, both of these were and still are crucial for our survival as individuals and as a species. Hunter gatherers needed to constantly switch between noticing potential dangers in their surroundings and keeping in mind what they were trying to achieve (like hunting a deer). The same happens when we drive – the ventral attention system makes sure that we are aware of our positioning on the road and the actions of other car drivers, but the dorsal attention system doesn't let us get too carried away and switches our focus back to where we are trying to get to and the roads we need to take to achieve that. In the same way, when I work on this chapter, my dorsal attention system keeps me on task, which is crucial in order to get any work done, but my attention naturally needs to switch to the ventral attention system just in case there has been a fire in the kitchen or my daughter has woken up and is crying her eyes out. The same switching between these two systems causes issues in our performance as well, especially if one network gets carried away. Imagine you are trying to create a logo for your company; you feel truly excited about it and spend hours looking at different images and torturing Adobe Illustrator. You get so focused that you don't even realise that the entire working day has gone. That would not be a problem if you didn't need to deliver a seminar to your client tomorrow. Of course, having a nice logo might have helped to represent your company better on the slides; however, now you have a logo, but no content… In addition to that, you haven't eaten or drunk anything so you are feeling very moody now (remember, lack of nutrients and overusing your PFC is likely to switch you to mammal-brain-dominant thinking) and have got a headache. To make matters worse, you go upstairs to grab some food and make a snappy comment to your partner, who is now upset. And that's all due to being lost in the single-focus dorsal attention system and the depletion of the PFC.

Let's look at an alternative scenario. You sit down to work, but there are some pretty birds outside and you stare at them for a while. Then you start to feel a bit peckish so go and make yourself a cheese sandwich. You sit down to write, but then, surprise, surprise, you realise that you are a bit sluggish and sleepy, so go and make yourself a strong cup of coffee. With caffeine rushing in your bloodstream you get a sense of urgency and light anxiety (as we discussed in Chapter Two, our emotional states can adjust based on body states, especially changes in heart rate such as those caused by caffeine) so you decide to check your emails, just in case somebody desperately tried to contact you. Of course, there are loads of emails waiting to grab your attention and you get drawn into checking and answering all of them. Then you realise you need to go to the toilet, which gives you a chance to check your social media while you're there (let's be honest, most of us do use our phones while on the toilet). Seeing the newsfeed, you realise you are not up to date with current affairs and start catching up on that. Then you realise that you need to go and take over the childcare or start cooking dinner. So how much productive work have you done today?

I know finding the right balance is tricky and we find all sorts of justifications as to why we need to do all of these other jobs or why having a perfect logo is important. But, in all honesty, would you like to get the presentation for your client done? If the answer is yes, let me share with you one of the most useful techniques I have come across for attention training, called the Pomodoro Technique (by the way, if the answer was no, still keep on reading, as we will discuss motivation and procrastination after this). This time and attention management technique was created by Italian coach Francesco Cirillo (2016) and named after a delicious Italian salad, where slices of tomato (*pomodoro* in Italian) are interspersed with slices of mozzarella cheese. Tomato slices represent the intervals of focused work on *one task* while mozzarella portrays unstructured or resting time, where you can do whatever you like. This method helps both people who tend to get overly focused on one task, and the ones who struggle to keep their attention on the task at all. The duration of time spent on the task can be chosen based on the difficulty of the task, the individual's current attention span and the state of the body and mind (so I would choose only 10–15-minute task intervals if I was really tired or feeling down).

When I was writing my PhD thesis, I would start my day with 45 minutes' writing straight after my morning coffee (I wasn't allowed to check emails or have a shower before that), then I would use my 15-minute break to take a quick shower and get dressed. After that, I would write for another 45 minutes, which if completed successfully was rewarded by a 30-minute break during which I checked my emails or went to the corner shop to get ingredients for my lunch. That was my minimum writing time for the day and I could then get on with all the other tasks I needed to complete. For some of them I used the Pomodoro Technique, while for others I didn't. It doesn't have to be strict, otherwise it creates too much stress. If I were to use shorter intervals (let's say 25 minutes), I would just need to do more of them. It's important that you break your task into small, manageable chunks and have everything that you need to work on it ready, so you can use the Pomodoro time to focus only on the task itself. For example, I would break the chapter I was working on into small sub-chapters and then break each of them down further into smaller topics to discuss as separate tasks. Each sub-chapter would normally take me two, sometimes three, 45-minute Pomodoros to complete. Also, focusing on the time spent writing rather than the number of words or level of completion of the task felt rather liberating and made me more in tune with the state of my PFC. Some days, I could get lots done in those two Pomodoros, while others not so much, but it still counted as success as long as I focused on doing only that task for the time set. When the time is up (please be sure to put a timer on, as our perception of time is not accurate), make sure to take a break even if you are close to finishing the task. During the break, do whatever you like and just go back to the task after the break. Unstructured time is crucial to replenish your PFC and to avoid so-called ego depletion which we experience if we are too strict with our working routine (that just depletes your PFC and doesn't give the glia cells a chance to clear out the neurotransmitter mess made during the activity phase). Of course, to go through the Pomodoro Technique, you need to be motivated about the task, so let's now look into the motivation aspect of productivity.

Increasing motivation

Needless to say, a big part of getting things done is the desire to do them. This especially applies to tasks that require persistent effort and troubleshooting. When we don't see a point in doing something we will not persevere, we will find all the reasons why we can't achieve it and, to put it bluntly, be useless at it. That applies to work, personal life and free time. For us to feel motivated, the activity has to 'tickle' the reward centres of our brain. Reward centres are part of the mammal brain complex and consist of the ventral tegmental area (VTA), which detects potential pleasure, and the nucleus accumbens (NAcc), where the feelings of pleasure, motivation and joy originate after it receives dopamine from the VTA. Reward centres, similarly to the amygdala, create bias attention, but this time with things that can lead to a positive experience – delicious snacks, interesting movies, people we are attracted to – and in general with situations where we have experienced pleasure in the past. Interestingly, we get a lot more dopamine if the outcome is not guaranteed, therefore, more challenging projects or unpredictable situations cause bigger rewards. As we have discussed before, the VTA is also connected to the PFC, which mediates decision-making, controlling attention and, in the pursuit of a very strong desire, temporarily deactivating rational thinking (if you have ever made stupid choices when you were sexually aroused, you now know which connections of your brain to blame). However, this connection is bidirectional – our thoughts alone can cause the feeling of pleasure. To experience that just close your eyes and either remember or imagine the most amazing day you have ever had or can think of.

This comes in handy when we talk about motivation – our perception of the importance of the task mediates how much we enjoy doing it. If I tried to do something that felt unimportant to me according to my highest values, such as keeping up to date with political affairs, even with my best intentions, I would struggle to find time to do it. My attention would drift away when doing it and I would not be able to retain the information easily. But if I was asked to deliver a neuroscience seminar on how the current political situation affects people's mental wellbeing, I would suddenly be a lot more motivated, as that is aligned with my highest values.

Given that we have the power to use our PFC to change our perceptions, let's now take something that I might not feel very motivated to do – marking student essays at the university where I lecture. I can increase my motivation for doing this task by linking it to my highest values. The more links I find, the more inspired from within I will feel in doing that task. So how would marking student essays benefit my top three values?

- If I marked them efficiently, I would have more time to spend with Emilija.

- Being good at my university job (which marking is part of) means I would be much more likely to get a permanent post, which would create financial stability for our family.
- If we had financial stability, Matthew would not need to work as hard, so he could spend more time with Emilija and take her on exciting outdoor adventures.
- Having more financial stability would allow us to provide the best education for Emilija.
- Having a more stable income means I would finally be able to buy Matthew his dream watch as his next wedding anniversary gift!
- By being efficient at marking, I would have more time for creating engaging and informative lectures for my students.
- In providing students with valuable feedback on their essays, I would help them on their journey of learning and perhaps some of them might even choose to do their MSc or PhD thesis with me.
- Having a team of great MSc and PhD students would enable me to create meaningful applied-neuroscience research experiments on relationships and I could write a second book about that.
- Being good at my job (which marking is part of) means I would be able to progress in my career to senior lecturer, then reader and then maybe even professor, which would increase my calibre as an author of future books.
- By having a great academic career, I would perhaps inspire Emilija to find a career that feels meaningful to her.

I could continue this list linking marking student essays with even more things that feel meaningful to me: being a great mum, being a good wife, having a happy family, doing interesting research, delivering impactful lectures, writing books that can help people achieve meaningful change, helping people learn and develop their thinking and so on. If you have an important task that you feel reluctant to undertake, I would suggest you write a list of the benefits of completing that task. If you want to take it even further, write another list: the negative consequences in the areas that are important to you of not doing the task. My list would look like this:

- I would lose my job as a lecturer and not be able to create and deliver impactful lectures and share my love of learning with students.
- I would set a bad example for Emilija.
- Matthew would need to work even harder, which could cause him health issues.
- With Matthew working so hard, he wouldn't be able to spend much time with Emilija, and she would grow up without a proper father figure and seek relationships with emotionally unavailable men (nooooo!).
- In procrastinating over my tasks, I would not be practising what I preach in this book, which would make me feel guilty and I would start procrastinating over writing this book.
- With delays in writing resulting from that, my publishers would cancel their contracts and all of my work would be wasted.

As you can see, I am amplifying the impact of procrastination in a way that the mammal brain can understand so as to cause an unidirectional movement – to do the f*cking marking! OK, with that in mind, I shall go and mark five essays and will be back once I have completed that.

Tackling procrastination and reducing stress

I am often asked in my seminars if procrastination always originates in a lack of motivation. Although that is sometimes the case, the causes of procrastination can be a lot more varied. First, procrastination follows the same habit loop we discussed in Chapter One. It starts with a trigger that sets procrastination off, then an action – doing anything but the task – which leads to a reward, and temporarily forgetting about the task. The most common triggers are lack of motivation, feeling overwhelmed by the task, not knowing where to start (particularly with long-term tasks such as writing a book/thesis, doing yearly accounting, renovating a house), fear of failure (some authors talk about fear of success as well) and fear of change or the unknown (What will I do when I finish my degree? Maybe I will just drag it out for longer). Based on the triggers, and on what needs we are meeting with our procrastination habit, we can divide procrastinators into six groups. The solution for each type is slightly different too.

Also, remember that every habit meets some needs, mostly one of these: safety, significance, love/connection, variety, growth, and contribution beyond yourself. The first three needs can be called mammal brain needs, as they are crucial for the ancient centres to feel calm and safe. If these needs are not being met to a sufficient extent, we often act irrationally, and that's not surprising – the mammal brain is not rational! If we feel stupid for procrastinating in a ridiculous way and can't seem to get a grip on it, it simply means that the mammal brain is running the show. So we need to identify what exactly is happening – What are the triggers? What needs am I meeting with my procrastination? What could be a better way to meet these needs? That will be the case for all six types of procrastinators, so let's dive in.

1. *Perfectionist procrastinators* want results to be *perfect*. This perfection often meets the needs of safety and significance. Sometimes, though, there are limits to time, energy and human physiology, making the expectations perfection-ists set themselves unattainable. Needless to say, that

overwhelms perfectionists and triggers a mammal brain response – avoidance of the task. To fight that, perfectionists need safety and significance in a different way. One method that I find helps perfectionists is the Pomodoro Technique we have discussed before, where we spend a well-defined period of time on the task and then have a break. This switches the focus from the perfect results to the time you spend on the task. Also, taking a break helps many people to keep perspective and not get carried away with the details. The aim for perfectionists is to learn to celebrate completion rather than perfection. While I am writing this book, I cannot edit it before I finish the first draft of all the chapters. I write about 1,000 words a day and can only use my current knowledge in the writing. Polishing and editing will come once I have completed the whole draft. This rule prevents me from spending hours rewriting and editing the text, doing lots of research and ending up hating writing this book. So in general, focusing on producing the first imperfect draft and postponing optimising it until later can help to tackle perfectionistic procrastination.

2. *Worrier procrastinators* mainly seek *safety*. With underlying low self-esteem, this type of procrastinator gets triggered by various fears: fear of failure, fear of success, fear of change, fear of the unknown, fear of judgement/criticism and so on. These fears easily trigger the amygdala, setting off irrational habits which lead to safety behaviours such as eating sugary snacks, talking to colleagues, smoking, drinking alcohol, watching TV, browsing social media. It often leads to a vicious cycle, with mounting pressure as the time left to complete the task runs down, triggering the amygdala into avoidant behaviours even more. A few things that can help worrier procrastinators include getting

a support team to build more safety, having a personal coach to work on underlying self-esteem issues, meditation and exercise or other stress-reduction techniques to calm the amygdala down. The Pomodoro Technique can also be useful for this type of procrastinator as it takes the focus off the results, but the danger is that worriers can easily beat themselves up for not managing to keep to the task during the Pomodoro stage, so lots of amygdala calming is required before even starting that.

3. *Dreamer procrastinators* seek freedom and variety. They often have a low threshold for boredom and get easily distracted if the tasks are monotonous and especially if they require sustained effort over a long period of time. Dreamers often have a strong *optimism bias* – they underestimate how long tasks will take and overestimate their own abilities. This leads to setting unrealistic goals and the inevitable failure to achieve them. With accumulated failure, dreamers build a resistance to working on the task and keep accumulating more work for the shorter period of time left, which feels more and more overwhelming. Dreamer procrastinators achieve most when they have a good accountability system, so with one of my PhD students we have a 30-minute phone call each week where we discuss whatever she has achieved that week and set the goals for the next week. Performance coaching, which can help to break the big task into manageable chunks and set realistic timelines, is also helpful. Also, dreamers can benefit greatly from gaining awareness of their *real* performance – if your goal is to call 30 potential clients this week, ask yourself: how many clients did you actually call last week? If it was three, then the highest goal for this week can only be four, as unrealistic targets will just get you into the same old trap. If you want to write 1,000

words a day on your blog, ask yourself how many words you currently manage. If it is 100, then 1,000 words is a ridiculous target – just write for five more minutes. If you manage that, add another five minutes after a short break.

4. *Defier procrastinators* have a strong sense of identity and they resist doing anything that doesn't fit their values. They get significance from being the way they are, so they need first to see the point of doing that task. They could achieve that from the exercise we discussed before – write down 50 benefits of doing the task related to your true top three values and then add 50 negative consequences of not doing the task for your highest values. This often helps defiers to get unstuck, but in some cases where these patterns originate from early childhood dynamics with caregivers (we will discuss this in more detail in Chapter Eight), deeper inner work is needed. This can be achieved through therapy or life-coaching sessions.

5. *Crisis-maker procrastinators* have a low threshold for boredom and need a constant rush to feel alive. They often have a big need for variety, and low dopamine levels (some might even have diagnosed or undiagnosed attention deficit hyperactivity disorder) and therefore need a sense of urgency to make them feel anything. Adding other dopamine-inducing activities to their lives (thrilling sports such as rock climbing or mountain biking) can help them to elevate their dopamine levels. Also, adding intermediate deadlines and working with a team, especially in a high responsibility role, can help as well. Other activities such as meditation, yoga and mindfulness can gently increase dopamine levels and retrain the brain for a slower pace too. Also, these activities can help if these thrill-seeking behaviours originate from a desire to run away from haunting emotions. Needless to

say, in the cases of severe past experiences causing emotional escapism, deeper inner work with a therapist with relevant credentials might be needed too.

6. *Over-doer procrastinators* place a very high value on helping others. They take tasks on, never saying no in order to meet the needs of connection, safety and significance. Given that this habit feeds so many needs, it's a very hard one to change. Before we even start, we need to think of alternative ways to meet the connection (maybe finding people who wouldn't take advantage of that trait? Time with family and friends? Having a good support team?). The second step is to learn to prioritise and delegate. In his book *The Seven Habits of Highly Effective People* (2020), Stephen Covey discusses the technique of four quadrants, which can be really handy here. Take a piece of paper and draw two lines crossing each other to create four quadrants. Write all the tasks you do and score each of them (on a scale of 1–10) on two measures: importance and urgency. Put all the tasks that are important and urgent into the top left quadrant (1), and the important but not urgent into the top right quadrant (2) – both these quadrants are the ones you want to focus your efforts and time on. The bottom left quadrant (3) contains non-important tasks that feel urgent – they often grab our attention but we must make sure that quadrants 1 and 2 are taken care of before we jump on these tasks. The bottom right quadrant (4) includes all the tasks that are neither important nor urgent, therefore we must practise letting these tasks go. Over-doer procrastinators also need to learn to delegate and to say no. Quadrant 4 tasks can provide a perfect safe ground to learn to do that.

Summary of Chapter Four

In order to create a lasting change in our productivity, we need to remember these points:

1. It's important to allow your PFC to replenish itself. Taking frequent breaks, maintaining good sleeping habits, eating nutritious food and doing physical exercise you enjoy will give the neurons of the PFC a chance to recover and will increase your brain plasticity, creating agile thinking, focused attention and an improved memory.

2. To remember things well, we need to pay undivided attention and make sure to get some good rest afterwards.

3. The brain consists of two different attention networks: the goal-driven dorsal network and the stimuli-driven ventral network. A good balance between these networks is needed for sustainable productivity.

4. Multitasking drains our brain's energy, wastes time and impairs our performance, so we need to train our brains to focus on one thing at a time. That can be achieved regularly using the Pomodoro Technique.

5. Procrastination is a natural way for the brain to react if there are strong triggers affecting the mammal brain, such as lack of certainty, lack of support or any deep-rooted fears. We meet different needs when we procrastinate, so identifying these needs and meeting them in a better way will reduce the tendency to procrastinate.

CHAPTER FIVE

Changing Your Brain Health

In this chapter, you will learn:

- What brain chemistry is, and how it affects the way we feel.
- What brain chemistry is needed for sound performance, attention and the ability to switch off.
- How chronic stress affects brain plasticity, brain chemistry and our performance.
- Why we need to sleep and what happens if we are chronically sleep deprived.
- How gut health affects our brain chemistry and brain health.

By now, most of us know how to take good care of our bodies, in theory at least. But how can we take care of the organ where all life experiences begin and end: the brain? In this chapter, I cover what conditions help your brain to function at its best and what conditions are harmful to it.

Neurons in the brain 'talk' to one another in two languages – electrical signals, called nerve impulses, and small chemical molecules, called neurotransmitters, which help to bridge the gap between neurons. In the human brain, we have around 60 different neurotransmitters, each of which has a slightly different function. The balance of these neurotransmitters is very delicate and keeps changing based on our habits, the food we eat, the stress we experience, the amount of sleep we get, our emotional states and so on. In this chapter, we will get to know these neurotransmitters and learn how to balance them so we can enjoy a calm and sharp mind and reduce the likelihood of feeling depressed, anxious and burnt out, and performing poorly.

Neurotransmitters of good moods

Neurons are not joined with each other directly – there is always a tiny gap between them (called the synaptic gap), so electrical impulses, which neurons normally use to code information, cannot jump through it (just like your phone can't be charged if you don't properly plug it in). Messages are sent across the gap by chemical molecules called neurotransmitters. Different neurotransmitters have distinct functions but, ultimately, the balance between them determines our mood, attention span, memory, and even physical energy. Let's start by exploring the role of the main six neurotransmitters and then we will look at how their interplay makes us feel and function in day-to-day life.

Serotonin is a neurotransmitter that is crucial for putting us in a good mood, getting decent sleep, dealing with pain, and in general feeling OK about our lives. Levels of this neurotransmitter fluctuate during the day – we have most of it in the mornings, and it declines in the afternoons. Sleep allows levels of serotonin to be replenished and the cycle continues. If we don't get enough sleep, that process might be disturbed. Also, we need decent levels of serotonin to get good sleep, so it can easily become a catch-22 scenario with low serotonin causing insomnia, which in turn doesn't allow it to be replenished. Since we can't really get inside the brains of living people to measure neurotransmitter levels directly, we often rely on the remaining neurotransmitters called metabolites to measure it indirectly. This is how the link between depression and low serotonin metabolite levels (implying potential low levels of serotonin) was established. Moreover, modern depression drugs are called serotonin reuptake inhibitors (SRIs), which means that they make the existing serotonin last much longer in the synapses. Interestingly, Dr Robert Sapolsky (2018) found that with baboons, the levels of serotonin change based on status, with high-ranking male monkeys having significantly higher levels of serotonin, creating dominant poses and more confident behaviours. We can increase levels of serotonin with physical exercise, by spending time in nature, having physical contact, practising mindfulness and gratitude, and engaging in talking therapies. Not surprisingly, these are all the things that people with depression are encouraged to do. However, it's another catch-22 here – we need decent levels of serotonin to be motivated to do anything at all, therefore it's very difficult if not impossible to start doing these activities when in a deeply depressed state. What does help, though, is practising these activities regularly when in a fairly good state so that when we hit lows (which unfortunately we all do at some point), these health-promoting habits become second nature and are much easier to maintain, even if we don't feel great.

Another neurotransmitter crucial for motivation and zest for life is *dopamine*. When we eat a delicious lunch, watch an enjoyable movie or pick up the phone to call a good friend, dopamine is released in the synapses of the reward centres in our brains, creating a feeling of pleasure. Dopamine also creates a sense of motivation and a desire to repeat actions that triggered the dopamine release previously. Dopamine levels are increased when we anticipate a reward, especially if it is not certain. This makes us drawn to thrilling situations of uncertainty in relationships, exciting hobbies and risks in our professional lives. There are many things that can hijack the dopamine system – recreational drugs, sugar, caffeine, social media, procrastination – making it really hard to stop activities that induce such an intense pleasure. In fact, experiments with rodents have shown that if the reward centres in their brains (nucleus accumbens or NAcc for short) are stimulated by a small electrical wire after they press a lever, they get lots of dopamine secreted in their brains, causing an overwhelming sense of pleasure. Given that it is a much more intense sense of pleasure than anything else they have experienced, they get so addicted to pressing that lever that they ignore everything else. Left to their own devices, they keep buzzing themselves, causing the pleasure-inducing squirts of dopamine, and ignoring water, food and mating until they eventually die of starvation. The same effect was seen in epileptic patients who agreed to have electrodes inserted into their NAcc during the brain surgery they were undertaking to tackle their seizures. When surgeons stimulated their NAcc, the patients reported an overwhelming sense of pleasure and wanted it to be repeated over and over again, to the point that it was all-consuming and they lost interest in anything else. At that point the surgeons took the electrodes out and after a while they got back to their normal lives. That just demonstrates how powerful dopamine-inducing activities and substances are – they create the compulsion to repeat these actions even if they are detrimental to our own wellbeing. It is not a conscious process, making it really hard to stop the actions voluntarily (the bigger the dopamine kick created by a substance or activity, the harder it is to stop it). More constructive ways to trigger a dopamine squirt include ticking things off on your to-do list, having a fulfilling career, practising enjoyable hobbies, writing gratitude lists, meditation or being with people you find stimulating.

The third feel-good neurotransmitter is called *oxytocin*, which creates a sense of attachment, trust and love in relationships where there is enough predictability and safety, creating a strong emotional bond. Oxytocin is released when we make love, cuddle our partner, hug our kids or other loved ones, stroke pets or develop strong trust- and acceptance-based relationships in our personal lives and at work. Oxytocin creates a sense of bliss, relaxation and love, making these interactions truly enjoyable.

Now we will look at these mood neurotransmitters in real-life situations. To do that, let's visit Andrew again (remember that guy from Chapter One?). He wakes up after a long deep sleep late on Sunday morning. He lies in bed for a few minutes watching the sun-rays entering the room through the half-open curtain. His brain has good levels of serotonin, which allows him to feel that he's in a good mood (not super happy, just contented and positive). He slowly gets out of bed and joins his family having breakfast in the open-plan kitchen. His first cup of strong coffee and the granola with fresh strawberries (you see, a lot has changed since Chapter One) increase the dopamine levels in his brain, creating a sensation of pleasure. He sits his two-year-old son on his lap and takes the hand of his wife across the table. Physical contact with the people who are so dear to him increases his oxytocin levels, causing a feeling of overwhelming love and triggering caring behaviours towards them. Of course, that was a perfect morning for Andrew. However, it's not every morning that he feels like this, even after he has changed his habits dramatically. To understand the effects of these mood neurotransmitters to the fullest, let's go back to the previous week when the picture was very different.

Andrew wakes up at 7.30 a.m. on Sunday morning. He still feels tired and would give anything to stay in bed but his mind is restless – he has an important deadline at work tomorrow, which he feels completely unprepared for. He feels empty inside (low serotonin) and his heart is racing as he gets out of bed (due to adrenalin, which we will revisit later). He drags himself to the kitchen. He makes a strong cup of coffee but even the thought of food makes him feel sick. He goes straight into the spare bedroom/office and stares blankly at the laptop screen. After a few hours of work on his presentation, he is even more irritable – he doesn't seem to be getting good ideas, and feels sluggish and unmotivated (low dopamine). Hearing the voices of his family members in the next room, he just feels lonely and isolated in his own stressful pursuits and can't access the overwhelming sense of love he usually feels for them (low oxytocin). A very different morning indeed!

Neurotransmitters of good performance

In addition to a good mood and motivation, we need to be able to think clearly, remember events, focus on the task and supress unwanted thoughts. And that's where the other key neurotransmitters, glutamate, acetylcholine and GABA, come in handy.

Glutamate is the most common excitatory neurotransmitter in the nervous system, having a wide range of functions. It is crucial for any executive functions, such as working memory, long-term memory, planning, paying attention, talking, listening and pretty much anything mental we do (it is the most universal 'language' in the brain, with about 90 per cent of all synapses between neurons using it). Interestingly, when glutamate is secreted in the synapses it changes the blood flow of the nearby blood vessels, making sure that more oxygen- and glucose-rich blood is delivered in this region where it is needed. In other words, glutamate makes sure that neurons that are working hard have plenty of nutrients and oxygen to function. However, strangely, glutamate spill-out can also kill neurons, in what is technically called glutamate excitotoxicity. That, unfortunately, happens in the cases of physical brain trauma or ischaemic stroke. Chronic glutamate excitotoxicity has also been suggested to be one of the contributors to neuronal loss in neurodegenerative disorders such as Alzheimer's and Huntington's disease. It is still unclear, however, if high mental activity, such as working really long hours and constant overthinking, can lead to glutamate excitotoxicity in healthy individuals (as I mentioned before, we can't measure neurotransmitter levels in the brain directly so it is a hard question to answer). However, a large amount of excitation, caused by glutamate, could definitely create a restless mind, jumping from one idea to another, with an inability to stay focused on one task, and trouble switching off.

Another neurotransmitter, *acetylcholine*, allows your brain to control your muscles, making it crucial for any kind of physical movement. Moreover, it is a main neurotransmitter for the autonomic nervous system, determining the times when our bodies rest and replenish and when we deal with danger. More importantly for this book though, it creates the states of alertness and single focus, making it crucial for performance and engagement. In addition, it plays a major role in memory and learning, so this is another reason to aim for good levels of it. Interestingly, acetylcholine is involved in some emotional responses, especially anger and aggression, as it helps to redistribute the energy resources of the brain, makes us super alert, and makes us focus on what is relevant to the situation. Last, but not least, it is important for sexual arousal – so it has a rather varied list of functions.

Another vital neurotransmitter is *GABA* (gamma aminobutyric acid), an inhibitory neurotransmitter, which means that it dampens the activity of neurons. Good levels of GABA are important to reduce the amount of thoughts we have to avoid mental overload. It also regulates our levels of anxiety, helps us to see things clearly, block out the background noise, and control our movements. The clearest example of a lack of GABA can be seen when people experience epileptic seizures – the whole body goes into spasm, as there is overwhelming amount of electrical activity rushing through the brain. In a healthy state, GABA reduces that so we have selective focus and clear thoughts, and can control our attention and actions. Lack of GABA causes chronic anxiety, stress and insomnia, and can contribute to depression (in fact, some people with depression have low levels of GABA, as measured by GABA metabolites in urine).

During Andrew's bad morning, when he has to prepare for his presentation, the balance of these neurotransmitters is not in his favour. Decent levels of glutamate to start with allow him to remember what tasks need to be done, critically assess the next steps and plan the day accordingly. However, with his lack of sleep and underlying worry, his glutamate levels start to ramp up, causing restlessness and impatience and an inability to think ideas through. At the start of the morning, his GABA levels are high enough to help him focus on the relevant work, but they can't do it with heightened levels of excitation due to excessive worry. Anxiety starts building up, which makes matters even worse, compromising Andrew's ability to think rationally and increasing his reactivity. Although acetylcholine created high alertness at first, it soon leads to more irritability and a lower threshold for anger. Next thing we know, Andrew is caught up in a vicious cycle of mammal-brain-dominant thinking, stopping him getting things done, and not allowing him to join his family for a relaxing time. So what can be done to restore this neurotransmitter balance?

First, we want to increase his levels of GABA to give Andrew a chance to dampen unwanted mind chatter. The best ways to do that include light physical exercise such as walking, jogging and especially yoga. Mindfulness, focusing on breathing and any meditative practices can greatly help with that as well. However, it is almost impossible to do it when we are already caught up in overly high levels of excitation. Therefore, Andrew needs to start his day with ten minutes of breathing exercises or meditation. After working for 45 minutes, he can take a 15-minute break to walk around the garden or at least walk around the house to get his body moving and disrupt the overthinking process. If Andrew has a tendency to get in that state, he will benefit from modifying his diet – avoiding sugary snacks and drinks, limiting caffeine, eating food high in glutamic acid (oats, bananas, nuts, broccoli, spinach, potatoes) and taking magnesium supplements. If he struggles to switch off before bed (thus impairing his sleep quality), he could have a cup of camomile tea or a glass of water with a few drops of passionflower tincture or other herbal remedies (valerian root, lemon balm, magnolia bark).

Second, he could control his levels of excitatory neurotransmitters. We can stop glutamate-containing neurons from getting overwhelmed by taking frequent breaks and doing breathing activities or physical exercise to switch off. Getting good sleep is crucial as well, as lots of 'repair' work is happening in the synapses during sleep, which we will discuss a bit later in this chapter. Last but not least, we can manage levels of acetylcholine with exercise and time in nature as well.

To reduce the component of amygdala thinking we need to do three things. First, we need to soothe the amygdala so it is not running the show. We can do that with breathing exercises, short meditations or a mindfulness break, such as Louise Hay's guided meditation (there are plenty of these on YouTube), a hug with our partner, a phone call with our mum or a close, soothing friend – whatever helps us to calm down.

Second, we can use our PFC with cognitive questioning techniques to educate our amygdala about the big picture. We can do that by asking questions such as:

- What's the worst that could happen?
- How important is that task in the big picture?
- What have I done well in this task or in my work in general lately?
- What were the causes that led to falling behind with this task?
- Did I set myself a realistic timeline?
- What can I learn from this experience for better planning in future?
- What are the advantages of things being as they are now?

To be fair, if you are already engaging in very negative mind chatter, these questions will just annoy you more. So, it is important to soothe your amygdala first.

The third part is to get your PFC back online by focusing on the process. We can do that by asking these questions:

- What exactly needs to be done?
- What is the most important part of this task?
- What are the small steps that need to be taken to achieve that?
- What is the most efficient way to achieve step 1?

Once you get into that way of thinking, you can use any insights from Chapter Four on productivity to get things done as best as you can within the time frame and energy levels you have left.

What happens to the brain during stress

That morning Andrew is getting irritated at not being able to produce a decent presentation for his work, his brain has produced the neurotransmitter called noradrenalin and his adrenal glands have created hormones called adrenalin and cortisol. All these chemicals are required to redistribute energy in the body and brain so it is prepared for the fight or flight response we spoke about in Chapter Two. Adrenalin increases our heartbeat and makes our breathing quick and shallow so we have plenty of oxygen-rich blood in our limbs for fighting or running away. Unfortunately, it doesn't save much energy for the smartest brain areas such as the PFC, which are required for staying rational, empathic and creative. Needless to say, that energy distribution within the body changes what things we are capable of during stress. We can only execute well-defined tasks we are familiar with, but score low on coming up with creative solutions to unfamiliar problems or truly understanding and empowering others.

Cortisol signals to your liver to break down glycogen storage into glucose and make lots of energy readily available for the muscles. Moreover, cortisol reduces the energy being consumed by the digestion, brain plasticity or the immune system, as these are non-essential functions in a crisis. As you can imagine, chronic stress can cause more harm than good, with a poorly functioning immune system making us more susceptible to infections, creating issues with our digestive systems and compromising learning and cognitive functions due to reduced brain plasticity. In fact, ongoing stress can even change the morphology of the existing brain cells. Chronic stress can 'trim the branches' of PFC neurons, making them less capable of forming connections, and compromising cognitive function. Meanwhile, the branches of amygdala neurons become lusher, making us quicker to react to danger but also creating negative mind chatter and stronger amygdala hijacking of the PFC during the threat.

But how can we manage stress in practice?

So it is clear that managing stress is a very important part of looking after your brain and getting things done. All the traditional advice we discussed in Chapter One on setting realistic expectations, doing the task early in the morning or after a break, taking frequent breaks and so on apply. However, there is more we can do – experiments with rodents have shown that our brain chemistry and levels of stress change dramatically, based on whether we have enough fun challenges in our environment or not. In the laboratory of Fred Gage (van Praag et al., 2000), rodents were placed in two large boxes – one just with water and food, and another one with a lot of tunnels, balls, and wheels to run and play on. Animals who were lucky enough to be in the fun box (called an enriched environment) were constantly busy, running around and playing with their mates. Animals in the boring box (called a standard environment) became less and less active, started sulking, didn't interact with each other much and were very susceptible to any stressors around them. Not only did these animals have a very different experience, but their performance started to diverge. Rodents in the enriched environment had increased brain plasticity, leading to higher cognitive abilities and reduced levels of stress. Animals in the standard environment started to decline in their brain plasticity, leading to poorer scores in the cognitive assessments and more stress. These differences were obvious even at the level of individual neurons – the PFC neurons of amused animals were lush and formed lots of synapses with other cells, while the same neurons of the bored animals had barely a few branches, making them less suitable to join the neural networks.

So what can we learn from this experiment? First, beware of boredom! If you find your work or life in general plain and boring, seek challenges that excite you. It can be anything – start a new venture, learn a foreign language, change your career, study neuroscience, strive for a promotion that feels meaningful. Whatever is high on your value list, do it. I know, I know, you might come up with lots of excuses now. We all have a limited amount of time, money and energy. But strangely, the more exciting and meaningful things you do, the lower levels of stress and more refined cognitive abilities you will have, which will equip you for getting more things done in the same amount of time. Another way to enrich your environment is travelling (if you are not into travelling, don't force yourself to do it, just fill your time with other meaningful hobbies). Levels of stress can also be managed by exercise, time in nature, and, especially, getting a good night's sleep, which we will discuss next.

Why we sleep

Another component of healthy brain functioning is getting enough sleep. A lot is happening during sleep – the PFC and many other areas of the neocortex are resting, while the mammal brain centres such as the amygdala and hippocampus (part of the brain that is crucial for long-term memory) are processing the events of the day. The brain areas we use mostly during the day need to rest and replenish, especially the PFC, which we use a lot during any given day. Neurons get loaded with neurotransmitters to be used for another day; damaged cells are either got rid of or fixed.

However, a lot more is happening when we sleep to ensure our sharp cognitive performance. First, the hippocampus runs through the information you encountered that day and selects what is worthwhile to keep in long-term storage. This process is called memory consolidation. If the hippocampus fails to consolidate memories, we simply lose the record of everything we learned during the day. That butterfly memory is obvious if we examine patients with hippocampus damage (also well depicted in the movie *Memento*). Professor Matthew Walker (2018) has proved that getting a full eight hours of sleep prepares our brain for efficient learning the next day. In his laboratory, people who were sleep deprived could only absorb 40 per cent of what the well-rested group were able to learn. For that very reason, when school start times were made one hour later in the USA, students on average attained significantly better grades in their tests. Also, in these schools, the death rates due to young people getting into car crashes were significantly reduced. In fact, lack of sleep is by far the most common risk in driving.

Sleep is crucial if we want to come up with creative solutions to a problem as the brain processes facts in a much more creative manner when we allow the mind to wander or sleep (so sometimes sleeping on the problem is indeed the best thing to do!). Needless to say, getting quality sleep is also important for emotional regulation, as the PFC needs good recovery to be able to keep the amygdala at bay. When we chronically lack sleep, it is far too easy to develop underlying anxiety and depressive thinking.

Moreover, in a small area near the hippocampus, called the dentate gyrus, new neurons are being created (neurogenesis), enabling life-long learning for us. These neurons develop and mature when we sleep, making them capable of taking on new tasks to ensure the acquisition of new skills and memories. Given this information, it is easy to understand why a lack of sleep causes poor memory, impaired decision-making, reduced willpower, poor emotional control, and higher levels of stress. Being chronically sleep deprived will run down your immune system, making it less capable of fighting infections. It will also compromise your hormonal system (men who sleep six hours as opposed to eight hours a night have the testosterone levels of men ten years older than them), fertility and cardiovascular system. That suggests that every system of the body repairs and replenishes its functioning when we sleep. When we talk about the benefits of sleep, it's not only the quantity, but also the quality that matters. When we sleep, we constantly shift between two main stages of sleep: the stage in which we don't dream, called the non-rapid eye-movement (non-REM) stage, and the one in which we experience dreams, called the rapid eye-movement (REM) stage, as our eyes flicker through it. REM is the stage of sleep when we process information in the form of dreams, and therefore it is crucial for learning and imaginative troubleshooting. Non-REM sleep is further divided into four stages, based on levels of awareness. In non-REM stages one and two, we can easily be woken up by noise or light, while stages three and four are called deep sleep, which are the most vital for our physiological systems to replenish. To give you an extreme scenario, laboratory rats that were constantly woken up, so they didn't reach deep sleep, died due to wear and tear to the vital organs.

To get better sleep, we need to have good sleep hygiene. Here are a few tips:

- Switch afternoon tea/coffee to non-caffeinated herbal teas, and also avoid soft drinks that are high in caffeine and sugar.
- Wind down activities in the evening – read books, walk in nature, do light physical exercise, cook dinner, do crafts.
- Reduce blue light exposure two hours before sleep – TVs, laptops and phones. As tempting as it is, if you are a poor sleeper, you need to find alternative entertainment.
- Limit alcohol intake – it does help you to fall asleep, but unfortunately doesn't allow you to get into deep sleep.
- Take frequent breaks during the day – getting ready for sleep doesn't only start when you go to bed, as all the activities of the day will have some influence on it. When we do a lot of glutamate-inducing activities, such as thinking, presenting, planning and multitasking, we shift our brain into an over-active state. If we don't have equally as much GABA to calm the brain down, we struggle to switch off. So, taking frequent breaks will help to reduce the excitability of your brain.
- Do GABA-inducing activities to help your brain to switch off – again, light exercise (a walk outside in nature or doing some yoga being perhaps the best ones!), mindfulness and guided meditation.
- Avoid excitatory foods and drinks during the day – sugar, or any food rich in simple carbohydrates, such as pastries, fast food and white bread. Avoid sugary drinks, and also sweeteners in food and drinks. It might be a good idea to make sure you eat enough protein (meat, fish, eggs or their vegan substitutes) with dinner so you don't get the late-night munchies.
- Listen to your natural day and night rhythm (your circadian clock). It might be tricky to start with as most

of us are not even aware of what times work for us since there are lots of activities and foods that stir up our brain chemistry. Also, some people who would naturally prefer going to bed late and waking up late simply cannot do it due to work or other commitments. Those who prefer to go to bed early might simply have too much to do in the evenings, especially if they have young families or other responsibilities on top of a full-time job. So, what we often end up doing is going to bed late and waking early, robbing our brains of well-needed rest and the processing of information during sleep. Most of us need around eight hours. Play about with your routine to train your circadian rhythms to fit around your responsibilities if you can't change them. If you can change your working hours to fit your circadian rhythms, that's even better. Keep a sleep diary and see what before-bed routine and what bedtime and wake-up times work best for you to get a good night's rest, and stick to them, even at the weekends if possible. By the way, catching up on lost sleep over the weekend doesn't seem to work in terms of fixing the damage done to your brain by the lack of sleep. Keeping your bedtime and wake-up time regular is one of the best things you can do to ensure good-quality sleep. It might take a bit of time to find a sweet spot, but I don't know any better way of your brain replenishing, recovering and rebalancing your brain chemistry for the next day.

Brain-gut health

Most of the brain chemicals we have spoken about start to be created in our gut from food we have eaten; therefore, our nutrition and gut health affect our neurotransmitter balance and play a significant role in changing our mood, energy levels, focus and cognitive abilities. The intermediate step between food being broken down and fully functioning neurotransmitters is called neurotransmitter precursors. GABA and serotonin precursors are created in our gut and then transported via blood to our brain. Brain blood vessels have much thicker walls to protect the brain from toxins and to maintain an intricate balance in brain chemistry (called the blood-brain barrier or BBB for short). That's the reason we cannot really change brain chemistry by ingesting neurotransmitters. The gut is somewhat selective as well, making sure that not everything we ingest gets into our bloodstream. That is crucial for regulating stable blood chemistry and controlling inflammation.

In some cases of food intolerance, such as celiac disease or dairy intolerance, or infection in the gut, the gut's ability to absorb nutrients and minerals from food we eat is altered. That also messes with the balance of the microbiome (the balance of different bacteria in your gut), dramatically changing the levels of neurotransmitter precursors produced and other building molecules that are needed for neurotransmitter production such as B group vitamins and magnesium. This often manifests as low energy levels, poor sleep, inability to focus on the task, reduction in performance, anxiety, depression and a higher susceptibility to stress (annoying, isn't it?!). In some cases, the walls of the gut might get so inflamed that they are less selective, causing so-called 'leaky gut syndrome'. That can cause small inflammation agents called cytokines to travel through the blood and create inflammation in other parts of the body. Sometimes, that can damage the walls of the BBB, allowing cytokines to access the brain and causing the inflammation of brain blood vessels. Inflamed brain blood vessels would then no longer be able to provide enough blood supply to the most advanced areas of the brain – the human brain, according to the Triune Brain model, but the PFC in particular. That would create a cloudy-head feeling, irritability, mammal-brain-dominant thinking, depression-like symptoms and, in some severe cases, schizophrenia-type symptoms. Interestingly, child neuropsychiatrist Lauretta Bender (1953) and authors of recent studies (Jackson et al., 2012) have noticed that patients with celiac disease showing these symptoms experience huge improvements in their condition after starting gluten-free diets. Of course, we must be mindful – not all schizophrenia and depression cases are caused by gut inflammation. But this does indicate that gut health can have a big impact (and in some cases a huge impact) on brain health.

So it's worth asking yourself these questions:

- Are there any foods that upset my gut? Keep a food diary and try to spot the links between what you ate and how you felt later.
- If I do get a cloudy head, what have I recently eaten or drank?
- Do I get a bloated gut after consuming dairy products?
- How does my gut react when I eat lots of wheat (bread, pastries, cereal, pasta)?
- How many portions of vegetables do I eat on average in a day?
- What are my sources of protein?
- How do my body and brain react the day after I have had alcohol?

Potential link between gut health and mental health (personal story)

I am not qualified to give you nutritional advice, but I do want to encourage you to observe how your body and brain react to different foods. It just might help you to gain some understanding of what does and doesn't work for you. For example, I am prone to migraine headaches. I have had them since I was eight and undergone all sorts of tests in search of the root cause, to no avail. During my PhD, I had a really rough patch when I averaged about 14 migraines a month. Needless to say, stress had a huge effect on me as I was doing experiments that were extremely challenging and success rates were soul-destroying. In addition to that, I was in a relationship with someone I cared deeply about but it was not leading to having a family and this was causing me constant inner turmoil. Last but not least, my family was going through rough times as my youngest sister was in a long-lasting battle with a serious illness. It was not the best few years of my life, as you can imagine.

That was also the time I started getting a very tender and almost constantly bloated gut. My brain felt itchy and my mind was in a constant fog. I couldn't think clearly, focusing on presentations during laboratory meetings was virtually impossible and I spent an awfully long time staring blankly at a screen when I tried to analyse data from my experiments. I couldn't perform well in almost anything. I was slow to react during my experiments, lacked the creativity and resilience to overcome setbacks and was really struggling with my data analysis. Everything felt like such an effort. I tried to eat more or less a balanced diet but there were significant changes in my digestion – each time I had dairy, wheat or sugar I felt sluggish and my brain would start getting itchy and cloudy within an hour. I tried to clear away the fog with coffee (four or five cups of espresso a day), which made me anxious and jittery. Also, I was nearly guaranteed a migraine if I had even a small glass of wine when out with friends. The things that seemed to help a bit were cycling, climbing, eating salads with prawns or salmon, and drinking lots of water with squeezed lemon.

Toward the end of my PhD I got a call from my family in Lithuania to share the sad news of my father passing away suddenly. I was utterly overwhelmed and didn't even know how to start processing the grief for my dad in such a state. I became depressed, and the first month was horrible. I could barely get out of bed or do any productive work. An intense pain was substituted with emptiness, anhedonia and apathy. I felt as if I had no reason to get up, but decided to force myself out of bed anyway.

My friend Filipa and I lived in the lovely Stoke Newington area at that time, with cozy Clissold Park a couple of minutes away. I came up with a challenge to run every morning (it wasn't much of a run – more like pathetic quickish walk, but I did it anyway). After my run, I jumped into a cold shower and made myself scrambled eggs with avocado and pumpkin seeds (adding smoked salmon on some days) with a cup of espresso (just one!). That combination often was enough to change my brain chemistry and enable me to cycle to work and get the experiment started. I would do the experiment as best as I could, interspersed with a quick lunch (my favourite options were quinoa with a salmon fillet, jacket potato with tuna or chicken with roast potatoes and broccoli), and one more espresso after lunch (making it two a day). At the end of the experiment I would cycle straight to the climbing centre to catch up and climb with my friend Maria. After that, we often had dinner together as well (usually in our local Turkish café, where chicken shish with rice and salad was my go-to meal). Did I want to do all that? To start with, definitely not – the only thing I wanted to do was stay in bed and play 'Two Dots' on my phone. To be honest, that's more or less what I did for the first two weeks. When I felt that I had a glimmer of energy I forced myself to go outside, as I knew I would feel better. On the days I couldn't run, I would get on my bike and cycle to work.

Once exercise increased my levels of acetylcholine I felt more alert. Whizzing through the London traffic increased my acute stress response (that's what we call 'good stress') with adrenalin and noradrenalin making my heart beat faster, expanding the blood vessels in my body and releasing glucose from my liver storage, giving me energy. My love for cycling increased my levels of dopamine, breaking the vicious cycle of anhedonia. Doing lots of exercise also had positive effects on my serotonin levels, helping me sleep better at night. That allowed serotonin precursors to be created in my gut while I was sleeping, which elevated my serotonin levels for the next day, making me a little less depressed. This altered balance of brain chemistry made it easier for me to do slightly more the next day, gradually unclenching the iron fists of depression. The most annoying thing I find about depression, though, is that vicious cycle – low levels of serotonin and dopamine draw us into inactivity, which in turn makes these levels even lower, and then it's harder and harder to see the point in (and to have the energy for) doing anything. Low levels of GABA make our minds restless and anxious, and prone to overthinking, draining valuable energy for mammal brain-dominant mind chatter. Overthinking then might cause glutamate excitotoxicity, which can damage neurons and cause an inflammatory response of the brain blood vessels, further compromising the blood flow to the PFC. Reduced PFC activity does not keep the amygdala in check, creating a lower threshold for anxiety, fear and anger and keeping us further stuck in a mammal-brain-dominant state. Chronic stress increases levels of cortisol and can compromise the digestive system, making good gut health much harder to maintain. Also, cortisol blocks the healthy maintenance of our immune system, making us more prone to infections. Last but not least, cortisol blocks brain plasticity, compromising our ability to learn, adapt and change, making doing the right thing and snapping out of depression even harder. We feel drained and isolated, and the amygdala points out every imperfection in the world. It's a bleak place to be.

In that state, we have three options: 1) Carry on as we are, but the odds of the brain chemistry changing by itself are low; 2) Take antidepressants to help the neurotransmitters work better (serotonin reuptake inhibitors cause the same serotonin to linger in the synaptic gap between neurons for longer, making it have a bigger effect); 3) Try to do something to alter our brain chemistry.

Of course, it can also be a combination of options 2 and 3. It is important to acknowledge that option 1 is a necessary stage on that journey. How long we stay there varies based on the cause of depression, the situation, our genetic predisposition and our individual brain chemistry in that state, what else is going on in the body and many other factors, making each case (and each depressive episode for the same person) incomparable to others (and there is no need to compare! Or, I suppose, compare if you like but it is just not fair on your brain to do so). Whatever your journey, it is what it has to be given all the factors mentioned above.

Here are some ideas for low-effort activities that could help to change your brain chemistry when you're stuck in a dark place:

- Get out of bed
- Have breakfast
- Have coffee (in the morning)
- Drink herbal tea (in the afternoon/evening)
- Drink water
- Read a book
- Watch an inspiring seminar/movie online
- Stroke a pet
- Call somebody
- Go outside
- Spend time in nature (avoid long commutes to get there at this stage)
- Go for a walk
- Do any form of low-effort exercise you enjoy (cycling, jogging and rock climbing work well for me)
- Spend time with someone who is easy to be with (it is best to avoid people who try to fix you as that might cause extra stress). Try to choose low-stress activities – a stroll in the local park, coffee in a cozy, quiet place, fixing a simple meal together)

- Spend time with little kids or pets – chasing my niece Julija around the park and focusing on looking after her worked well for me (remember oxytocin? It counterbalances the negative effects of stress on brain plasticity)
- Go to bed at roughly the same time each night
- Wake up at the same time each day
- Do crafts that you enjoy
- Doodle/draw or use colouring-in books
- Use the Headspace app for guided meditation or Louise Hay's meditation videos on YouTube, or similar alternatives
- Take supplements that work for you (I often take turmeric, B group complex, vitamin C and omega 3).

Of course, the list could be a lot longer and it has to include things that work for you, so I suggest making your own list and keeping it somewhere handy. It's crucial that you make this list prior to being in a devastating state as you simply won't have the brain capacity to come up with solutions. Also, if you can make it a regular habit to do some of the activities on your list (such as going for a daily walk/jog in the morning or developing good sleep habits), it will be easier to get back into that habit even if you are not feeling great – and that can help to keep the brain chemistry well balanced.

So now let's make another list – things *not to do* when in that state:

- Browse Facebook
- Go to very noisy and crowded places
- Take public transport (OK, this one is sometimes hard to avoid)
- Do very strenuous physical exercise
- Meet up with well-meaning friends who are trying to 'fix it'

- Meet up with a group of friends (this is OK sometimes, but can be overwhelming and much more draining)
- Drink alcohol
- Drink coffee late in the afternoon/evening
- Skip meals (it might be hard to eat a decent meal, so I would suggest at least having a small snack at the usual time of the meal)
- Lie in bed all day (it's OK on really bad days, but try to get out of bed as soon as you can)
- Read or watch the news
- Take on the tasks that can wait
- Do activities that stress you out (such as checking your bank balance)
- Eat food you know your body doesn't tolerate.

As in the previous task, I would suggest writing your own list of things that you know make you feel worse when you feel low. It is important that you don't allow your brain chemistry to get even more off-balance by doing things that cause you stress or upset. On a good day, these things won't matter as much but you don't have much of a buffer when your brain chemistry is out of whack, so it's best to be very selective in what you do and don't do.

Summary of Chapter Five

In order to look after your brain health, be mindful of the following points:

1. Doing constructive activities maintains a good balance of mood-creating neurotransmitters such as dopamine, serotonin and oxytocin.
2. The brain needs a balance between excitation and inhibition to be stable. Too much excitation will cause a restless

mind, distractibility, an inability to rest and ultimately poor performance. So, taking frequent breaks, meditating, exercising, spending time in nature and tweaking your nutrition will help you increase your levels of GABA to dampen glutamate-induced excitation.

3. The stress neurotransmitter noradrenalin and the hormones adrenalin and cortisol prepare your brain and body to escape danger, but steal energy from other functions, such as creativity, smart rational assessment, empathy, brain plasticity, and a healthy immune system and digestion. To look after your brain well, you need to manage your stress response.

4. To maintain a healthy neurotransmitter balance and help our brains recover and replenish, we need to sleep around eight hours a night. And no, five to six hours is not eight hours! So do everything you can to get good sleep. It's the best thing you can do for your brain.

5. Good gut health is crucial for absorbing nutrients from food, producing neurotransmitter precursors and keeping your blood-brain barrier intact. If there is anything causing an inflamed gut, it will inevitably give you issues with your neurotransmitter balance and brain health.

CHAPTER SIX

Changing Your Decision-Making

In this chapter, you will learn:

- Characteristics and brain areas of Kahneman's (2011) emotional decision-making System I and rational decision-making System II.
- The benefits and problems with decision-making System I.
- The benefits and problems with decision-making System II.
- The neuroscience of how emotions and rational thinking get integrated for sound decision-making.
- Embracing serendipity in decision-making.

Every day we need to make decisions: from small ones like what to eat for lunch, to which car to buy, what job to choose or whether our partner is the best match for us. For many years, there has been a big misconception that in order to make sound decisions we need to rationally assess the pros and cons of each option. This leads to many people being utterly stuck in indecision (also called analysis paralysis), especially if faced with a large number of things to choose from.

Recent neuroscience research not only suggests that emotional intelligence helps us to make better personal decisions, but also that an emotional component is necessary for us to make any decisions at all (most of these experiments have been performed by Antonio Damasio (2006) and are described well in his book *Descartes' Error*). In fact, the new emerging paradigm is that we make decisions emotionally and use our rational mind to justify them to ourselves. In this chapter, we will discuss both decision-making systems, as described by Daniel Kahneman (2011) in his book *Thinking, Fast and Slow*: the emotional and quick System I (also called 'making decisions by heart' or 'following gut instinct') and the much slower rational System II. Combining Kahneman's work with the latest neuroscience research, we will look at the benefits and drawbacks of different decision-making systems and examine the best ways to incorporate their wisdom so we can learn to make the best decisions, overcome the traps of indecision and be aware of our biases.

Emotional (System I) and rational (System II) decisions

Any time we have to make any decision at all, we can choose a few approaches. First, we can choose what 'feels right', also called following our 'gut feeling' or 'making decisions by heart'– what Daniel Kahneman calls decision-making System I. These decisions rely on being aware of how you feel about each of the options and choosing what you are drawn to. Rationally, it might not make the best sense, but your 'gut instinct' or 'heart feeling' is pulling you that way. A good example of that could be being drawn to somebody and not exactly understanding why that is, but wanting to spend more and more time with this person. Second, we can weigh the pros and cons of each choice rationally and choose the option that scores the highest; this is Kahneman's decision-making System II. In this way, choosing a partner or even a friend would consist of thinking through all the aspects that you want in the relationship and assessing people you know based on these criteria. Both of these systems have distinct advantages and shortcomings, making a combination of them crucial for overcoming biases and indecision and avoiding past mistakes. But let's look at the brain mechanisms of each system in order to gain a greater understanding of what each of them is useful for.

Decision-making System I: The gut feeling

First, System I relies on subconscious information, which is provided by the mammal brain. If you remember from previous chapters, the mammal brain does not require much energy and can processes information very fast and effortlessly. However, the mammal brain heavily relies on past experiences. It creates positive or negative emotions as the result of familiarity to the events that caused you similar experiences in the past. If we go back to the example of being drawn to somebody, it's not random. Your mammal brain compares the looks, mannerisms and even smell of that person to other people you have encountered in the past. If this person subconsciously reminds you of somebody that hurt you in the past, the mammal brain will create anxiety and try to steer you away from that person. However, if that person subconsciously reminds you of somebody who was truly important to you in the past, even if you are not aware of that similarity, your mammal brain will trigger dopamine release in your reward centres, causing you to be drawn to him/her. In other words, System I is subjective and biased by your past experiences. This applies not only to personal preferences, but also to decisions we need to make in our professional lives. Malcolm Gladwell, in his book *Blink* (2006), describes a brilliant example from researcher Gary Klein: a case study of fire fighters. Fire fighters entered a burning building and tried to extinguish the fire source in the kitchen. Strangely, the fire was searing and wasn't giving in even after gallons of water were poured over it. Suddenly, the fire chief commanded everyone to leave the building. Immediately after the fire fighters were safely evacuated, the house collapsed. So what did the fire chief have to say about his decision? 'I don't know why, but I had this gut feeling that something was not right,' he replied, shrugging his shoulders. What he learned later retrospectively helped to solve the puzzle of where that feeling originated. The fire source was not in the kitchen as they had thought but in the cellar, right under the kitchen. The fire chief admitted that he could remember things being different about this fire – there was a lot more heat in the room than such a seemingly small fire could create. Also, there was a strange roaring noise, which must have been from the fire underneath. What the fire chief's mammal brain knew was that this fire did not match the heat distribution, sound and response to water of any other similar kitchen fires his team had successfully extinguished in the past. The amygdala created a danger-warning signal, which he was quick enough to act on. Had he used his rational brain and tried to understand what was going on at that moment, he and his team would have likely been killed. Would you and I be able to make such a judgement in that situation? Most likely not, as we don't have any experience with what a normal kitchen fire is like so there would be no valuable information held in the mammal brain for us to compare that situation to (so for us this rule would be smart to follow – if there is a fire, just leave the building). As you can see, decision-making in System I is fast, effortless, relies on past experiences (for better or worse) and includes our emotions in the equation. The biggest issue for this system is the inability to communicate the thinking process behind it (as it mainly happens in the subconscious centres), the cognitive biases and the inability to get away from unhelpful patterns of the past, which we will discuss in greater detail later.

Decision-making System II (rational thinking)

System II is based on a rational assessment of the situation. It relies heavily on the PFC processes, and going through the pros and cons of each solution to weigh them against each other. To come back to the example of choosing a partner, your PFC will need to go through all the aspects that are important to you in a relationship and measure each person you are considering against these. In doing so, the PFC consumes lots of energy and requires undivided attention, making it an effortful and time-consuming process. Unlike System I, we can rationalise and verbalise our thinking as the facts we base our rational decision on are easily accessible for the PFC. Issues arise when an emotional component is also required for the situation to be favourable. Have you ever tried to use this approach for choosing your ideal partner? You write down a shiny list of criteria your perfect match needs to meet on paper. One day, your friend says, 'I have found Miss/Mr Right for you based on the list you showed me. Would you like meet her/him?' 'Of course!' you reply. You meet, have a pleasant time, but it just doesn't feel right to go any further with it. OK, if you were smart, you might have included 'chemistry' or 'feels right' as separate criteria on the list to merge both decision-making systems. But as you can see, System II alone might not produce a favourable outcome on its own if happiness, which is a *feeling*, is what you are after. The same applies with career choices – probably the most common type of client I have worked with were very successful men and women, who chose sensible careers and worked hard to reach the top only to find themselves depressed, unhappy and lacking meaning in their jobs. So in the case of happy relationships and meaningful careers, there often is a need for input from the emotions-based System I, which we will cover later on.

On the positive side, using the rational approach can help us to overcome past mistakes or our character shortcomings. Being rather impulsive by nature, I need to use this system a lot to avoid rushed decisions, making me a better driver, a more consistent parent and preventing unnecessary purchases. But there is another issue with using the purely rational System II approach: analysis paralysis. This is where there are too many things to choose from. I get this when I am shoe shopping if none of the options stand out enough to stack the benefits of one pair of shoes over others. So in that case, again, emotional input from System I is needed to create a preference and get us unstuck. Let's look now at the issues with System I and System II in order to come up with insights into how to best merge them both for sound decision-making in the future.

Unconscious biases

The term unconscious bias indicates that processes leading to decisions are based on mammal brain centres, making it impossible for us to be truly aware of them. Tversky and Kahneman (1974) called these quick subconscious assessments heuristics – mental shortcuts, based on the past experiences, that allow quicker decision-making, but can unfortunately lead to biases. In order to gain that knowledge and self-refection, we will go through the most common types of these biases and we will discuss practical ways to challenge them.

First, *familiarity bias* occurs as our brains are trying to predict the most plausible outcome based on similar situations from the past. If you have owned a dog of a certain breed, you naturally attribute the traits of your dog to other dogs of that kind, helping you to make a snap judgement as to whether you should protect your child from this dog or let her stroke him. Unfortunately, we do that with people as well, creating stereotypes, race-based discrimination and gender-based expectations of behaviour. The only thing that can help to reduce this bias is exposure to new situations or people we are biased towards until it becomes familiar. Being exposed to groups of people we stereotype or reading books or watching movies about them can help to alter these beliefs, but that is, unfortunately, a slow process, as the mammal brain processes take time to adjust. If you want to assess what familiarity biases you posses, I would suggest taking a Harvard Implicit Association Test (https://implicit.harvard.edu/implicit/takeatest. html). I do that test with my university students and they are often shocked to find out that they have implicit biases around gender, age, culture and sexuality, although this doesn't match what they think about these topics rationally. And that is a very important point – sometimes our rational and subconscious information doesn't match. Subconsciously we all are unfortunately biased based on our upbringing and what we have been exposed to most frequently, so being aware of these biases could help us to adjust our decision-making accordingly (using rational System II) to make sure we come up with a fair outcome.

To make matters worse, our biased perception (as we discussed in Chapter Three) creates a *confirmation bias*, making us subconsciously notice evidence to support our beliefs. Imagine if you were watching a person on the street and you didn't notice anything unusual about that person. Suddenly you are told that this person has just been released from jail. What traits do you start noticing in this person's behaviour? What if instead, you are told that this person is a genius, who is being considered for the next Nobel Prize? Would you start noticing completely different things about his/her behaviour? Nothing about that person has really changed, but your assumptions and perceptions have. It's crazy, but we do this all the time. Just being aware of which people we are biased towards and where that might have originated can help us to rationally challenge these beliefs.

We can use our PFC's rational thinking to challenge these beliefs. Let's say you have a belief that women are more empathic, making them more nurturing parents. That would naturally impact all the decisions you make in balancing your work and family life. It could impact the hiring decisions you make if you are recruiting and the opportunities you pursue if you are a young female with a dream to have children in the near future. In order to challenge this belief, we need to stack up evidence of the opposite. We can do this both by reading about or thinking about men we know who are very empathic and also thinking about women who are not very empathic and not very nurturing. We can also find evidence of activity-based plasticity and empathy – the more you do it, the better you get at it, creating yet another argument that maybe the less empathic partner should do more parenting to get better at it. Also, we can challenge the idea that being more empathic is better for parenting, especially as children hit the terrible twos or teenage years.

So as you can see, there are lots of different approaches we can take with it. Feel free to choose one that resonates with you and challenge it rationally. Also, maybe your belief is completely different, so don't be offended by me using this example – I am biased by my own experience too, having grown up with a very nurturing and dedicated mum, and a father who was primarily focused on his work and playing chess. Again, I am not saying that one of them is better than another, just that my amygdala has made a record of what things have caused me pain and what has caused me safety and acceptance (activating the reward circuitry) in the past.

Another type of bias – *egocentric bias* – is similar to confirmation bias in the sense that it is based on skewed perception, but this time we tend to overvalue what we have and undervalue what we gave up. For example, new car owners tend to value the car they have chosen over other cars they have considered, even if before they might have ranked these cars similarly. The same applies with ex-partners – we tend to see them as much worse than they objectively were, and couples who choose not to have children see a lot more benefits in that choice when they compare themselves to those who have made an irreversible choice of having one or more children. Shall we challenge that bias? Not necessarily. Egocentric bias might have served as an adaptation to ever-changing living conditions to help people feel happy with what they have and not to dwell on the lost options, creating a better mental state and, in turn, better relationships and productivity. However, we must be aware of this bias when we discuss our choices with other people and not allow that to drive our advice to them.

Similarly, *optimism bias* causes us to overvalue our talents and abilities. This leads to 90 per cent of the population thinking that they are above average drivers (I am not!). This bias also makes us implicitly overvalue the likelihood of good outcomes and under-value the chance of bad consequences happening to us. That is the very reason we keep eating foods high in carbohydrates (some people do develop diabetes when they eat processed foods, but it is not going to happen to me), smoke (c'mon, lung cancer? Not me!), have unprotected sex or use recreational drugs. That is also the very reason that we still get married even though 50 per cent of couples end up divorced. Optimism bias might help to overcome past setbacks in suggesting that better things are waiting for you, making it a successful coping strategy in some situations. However, people with high optimism bias are more prone to leaving tasks to the last minute, reckless driving, taking unnecessary risks and developing chronic health issues due to a poor lifestyle. If you want to challenge this bias in your productivity, you can use your rational mind to examine if your judgement is sound or skewed by unrealistic optimism – how long did it take you to perform this task in the past? Who can you ask for feedback for improvement? How many words did you manage to write in a day on average last week?

The last one on the list – *anchoring bias* – influences our decisions and even behaviour based on previous exposure to seemingly unrelated objects, words or numbers. In the study of Chapman and Johnson (1999) participants were asked to write down the last four digits of their social security before they entered a bidding war. Surprisingly, people whose four digits of their social security number were highest put the highest bids, and the ones with lowest numbers – lowest bids. Even more surprisingly, the temperature you are exposed to can change the way you judge a person's character. Researchers Lawrence Williams and John Bargh (2008) at Yale University asked a person taking part in their study to hold the researcher's cup of coffee when they were in the elevator. Some people were given an iced coffee to hold while others had a hot cup of coffee. Surprisingly, the temperature of the cup influenced the personality traits people assigned to the researcher. People who held a cup of iced coffee thought the researcher was distant and unapproachable, while people who held a hot cup of coffee thought the same person was warm and kind. As strange as it sounds, it makes sense from the brain's perspective as the same brain area, called the insula, processes physical warmth and the metaphorical warmth of personality. In their famous study, John Bargh and his colleagues (1996) showed that the words you are exposed to can even change your behaviour. People who were exposed to words associated with being old (such as slow, ill, wrinkles, grey) walked the corridor more slowly than the group who were exposed to the words associated with being young (such as energy, liveliness, speed).

Although System I offers speed and effortlessness in the decision-making process, it is prone to biases due to past experiences. Let's look now at System II as an alternative to overcome that.

Indecision

System II, based on rational thinking, allows us to have insights into the decision-making process, but it is rather slow, requiring knowledge of all the relevant variables to consider and the weighing up of the pros and cons. It is crucial to assess each scenario on the criteria that are important to you personally. One of my clients, Sophie, had begun to be very frustrated with the living conditions in her London flat. She was forced to rent a flat in a hurry after splitting up with her partner unexpectedly, so she just took the first half-decent option she came across, hoping to find a better one in the next three months. Can you guess what happened next? Three years later, Sophie was still in the same flat. As time wore on, she began to write extensive lists of the areas she might want to live in, criteria she had for the style of building and what the interior of her perfect flat would look like. She was also dithering over whether to get a one-bedroom flat just for herself or to share a two-bedroom flat with one of her friends. There were so many pros and cons of each of these options, it was becoming too exhausting to process. Moreover, Sophie couldn't assess some of these options properly, such as a flatshare with a friend, as she hadn't tried them in the past. Also, recalling the hassle of her last move, Sophie felt anxious to make the best choice so she wouldn't need to move again for a while. As the days slipped by, Sophie's preoccupation with these choices meant that she used escapism activities, such as a glass of wine and a movie in the evenings, to run away from the guilt and shame that she hadn't managed to make a decision. To make matters worse, Sophie's indecisiveness expanded into other areas of her life too, such as what to eat for dinner, which movies to watch and where to go on holiday. So let's look at the insights from neuroscience research in order to help Sophie to get unstuck.

Merging System I and System II

Neuroscientist Antonio Damasio (Damasio, 2006; Bechara et al., 1997) received a very interesting case – a successful lawyer had become permanently stuck in indecision about even insignificant choices he had had to make since he had undergone minor brain surgery. His wife had become very annoyed at him for not being able to choose a meal at a restaurant or for getting overwhelmed when deciding what time to go to the cinema, and took him to Damasio's office. After a thorough examination with cognitive tasks, Damasio couldn't find any impairments in his functioning as he scored very highly in all of the tests. As he had another patient coming soon, he suggested booking the second appointment the following week to continue the investigation. And that was when Damasio noticed something strange – the patient was going through different dates and times, naming the pros and cons of each option against traffic, other arrangements, levels of tiredness and so on, but simply could not commit to any of the options. After a brain scan, Damasio found that the connection between his amygdala and his PFC had accidentally been cut through during the previous brain procedure, making communication between these two regions impossible. This discovery led to Damasio starting decision-making research on other patients who had similar damage to their vmPFC, which is the part of the PFC that connects emotional inputs from the amygdala to the rest of the PFC. VmPFC lesion patients had odd behaviours – they were prone to gambling and taking risks, were impulsive, careless with other people and often struggled when they needed to make simple decisions.

In the experimental tasks, these patients not only had difficulty making choices based on personal preference, but their assessment of risk (assessed using financial gambling tasks) was severely impaired. In these tasks, the PFC was trying to figure out the best solution, while the mammal brain warned of financial loss (amygdala) or gain (reward centres). Therefore, good integration between rational and emotional centres was needed for good performance, which was unfortunately lacking for these patients.

This suggests that important choices in life require an emo-tional component, provided by the mammal brain centres, to be integrated with rational PFC assessment. Our day-to-day life involves making decisions on how to spend our monthly salary, which career options to pursue, who to date and even which foods and other health-related habits to indulge in. The rational mind can suggest good ideas based on the data it has accumulated, but can easily get stuck without the emotional input.

Each of us can, unfortunately, find ourselves sinking into indecision when we suffer with anxiety, depression, get exhausted or experience brain inflammation. Each of these causes influence the communication between the amygdala and the PFC. That also results in indecision, flatness and a lack of subconscious insight. Although there is not much we can do for patients with brain damage, we can incorporate some of these insights into other cases. If you are struggling with an episode of anxiety, depression or fatigue, postponing important decisions until a later date might be a good idea. However, in many cases, indecision can also be a learned response from the times when we have faced challenging decisions or when we have been penalised no matter what decision we have made (dammed if you do, dammed if you don't situations). If you struggle to make any decision, you have to start small – if you are shopping and can't choose which yogurt to buy, flip a coin. If you don't like it, you can buy a different one tomorrow. If there are ten yogurts to choose from and you can't even narrow the choice down, have an arbitrary rule, such as choosing the third from the left. In that way, you are trying to educate your mammal brain that many day-to-day decisions are not matters of life or death. If you have been spending lots of time considering what to choose, that just reinforces to your brain that this decision is very important. If you consult your PFC on that, it will most likely agree that which yogurt you buy doesn't matter too much. If you struggle to choose what to eat at a restaurant, have a go-to option for the times you feel indecisive – for me it is salmon fillet, and if they don't have it, I just ask them to bring me any kind of fish. On the days I feel in a good mood, I like to experiment with food and might order something that we don't often eat at home, like lamb tagine or sushi. So, an important part of making sound decisions or making decisions at all is observing your emotional state and adjusting your decision-making process accordingly.

So let's come back to Sophie. Her initial indecisiveness was caused by a difficult choice to make using purely rational thinking due to too many options and variables to assess with very little knowledge of each. After a while, that indecisiveness started to cause Sophie an emotional load – guilt, shame, sadness – as she was feeling foolish for being stuck in indecision. The stronger she felt these emotions, the more indecisive she felt, which permeated into many other choices, even trivial ones such as meals or evening activities. To resolve that, we need first to soothe Sophie's amygdala by validating her feeling of being stuck (I know, it is counterintuitive). She needed to learn about decision-making System II and that it was completely normal for her to be stuck given the amount of data her brain had to process. Also, she learned about the importance of the emotional amygdala input in getting her unstuck, triggering an 'aha' moment for her as she recognised that it had been a stressful period for her over the last few years, and a sound and calm amygdala had been pretty impossible for her to obtain.

So let's go to the next step. To get unstuck, Sophie needed to start with daily amygdala-soothing activities, like the ones we discussed in Chapter Two. After that felt like a sound habit, Sophie made a new list – the top eight things that needed to be in a flat for her to be happy. Then we ranked how her current place scored for each of these criteria. The majority of scores were below 5 out of 10, making an average of just a bit above 4. Then we brainstormed what the dream option would be where each criteria would score

9 or 10 out of 10. What would that flat look like? Where would it be? What would it be like to be there on a day-to-day basis? Lucy smiled – she knew exactly what the answers were. She had once been in a friend's flat in the Angel area, which would have been just perfect for her. Based on that, Sophie gave herself homework – to search through property sites to try and find a similar option. Strangely, that memory of a flat she really fell for helped her to add an emotional component to her rational thinking, getting her not only unstuck but also energised and motivated. She still needed to keep doing amygdala-soothing activities at that point, as guilt and stress can often throw us back into indecisive patterns. After some browsing, she narrowed down her search to four flats, which she arranged to view, and one of them was spot on. What did she have to lose, given that she hated the flat she lived in anyway? But the amygdala loves familiarity, so when it is running the show, it keeps us stuck in the same old places even if they are not good for us. Managing our moods and keeping the amygdala calm is a crucial part of sound decision-making.

Emotions are an intelligent subconscious summary of what does and does not work for you personally, therefore they are crucial for sound decision-making. Moods, however, can distort decisions as they reflect the brain chemistry fluctuations due to lack of sleep, changes in hormones, hunger, tiredness, nutrition and amount of exercise. The quantities of each neurotransmitter, as we have discussed in Chapter Five, change from day to day given all these measures. That can make us moody, anxious, aggressive, flat and hypervigilant. We can often mistake these moods for emotions, attributing the origin of them to the current situation (for example, career choice, relationship dynamics), pushing us to lash out or quit a situation on the wrong assumptions. However, jobs and relationships can cause emotions too, which usually change quickly when you are away from the situation. These are valuable for decision-making. Moods usually last longer, the onset is not clear and they feel diffused (don't have a clear source). Even happy moods can distort decision-making, as we tend to take bigger risks and have more pronounced optimism bias in these states. That can make us mess things up too – quit good jobs, start unrealistic businesses, ruin relationships. So the best time to make a decision is when you are well rested, in a balanced mood with a well-functioning PFC and have clear emotional input from the amygdala.

Embracing serendipity in decision-making

Of course, some decisions are complex and require breaking the long-term decision down into smaller timelines. In fact, this is an approach I've taken myself and many of my clients have also benefitted from. During my PhD, I found out that no matter how much I loved learning about brain mechanisms involved in human behaviour, the path of a researcher did not feel well suited to my personal preferences. I wanted to work with people and, in particular, help them by sharing neuroscience insights. I wasn't sure at that time what shape this would take, so I explored a few options. First, I created an applied neuroscience course for teenagers, called My Brain During the Day, and taught it as an extra-curricular subject for gifted pupils from disadvantaged backgrounds. I really enjoyed working with adolescents and was thrilled each time they shared that due to this course they could understand their emotional patterns and behaviour better. However, I had only six classes with students and the school setting provided further limitations. I then acquired a qualification as a business and performance coach from the university where I was doing my PhD, and I worked as an internal coach for university staff. That's when I started experimenting with merging neuroscience insights with coaching tools. After I completed my PhD, I continued this journey by starting my own business. A few of my clients, who knew about my seminars in schools, asked me if I could deliver similar seminars in their companies, universities they were working in or on their teacher training programmes. This branch of my business grew really quickly as I was getting repeat business and referrals. That, of course, was very time sensitive as there was growing interest in neuroscience in the business and education sectors. Soon I was asked to do public talks in London, and pretty quickly I was doing two or three fully sold-out public talks a week on subjects such as changing habits, emotions, brain health and relationships. Having a platform to share these topics allowed me to figure out which insights created the biggest change for attendees. I also started creating my own coaching tools, based on these neuroscience insights. This book is a combination of both paths that took me over five years to develop. Needless to say, I am happy and now share valuable topics with my students at university as well.

Could I have come up with this career path in 2015 when I was finishing my PhD? Definitely not! I knew I wanted to help people in a meaningful way, but didn't know at that point what format that was going to take. My career choice decision needed to be broken down into many mini-decisions:

1. Choosing to deliver seminars in schools – I knew I wanted to share neuroscience insights with non-scientists and this was the format that was available to me at that time.
2. Choosing to get a coaching qualification – I came across coaching incidentally but felt it was something that resonated with me.
3. Choosing to turn coaching into a full-time business – I was getting positive feedback when coaching university staff and started getting referrals to non-university peers. As I finished my PhD, I already had a few paying clients,

just enough to cover my expenses. I wanted to give it a go and come back to research as a back-up if that didn't work.

4. Launching seminar programmes for companies – this was something that was, again, somewhat circumstantial. I wouldn't have been asked to do it if I hadn't developed an applied neuroscience course for teenagers and if I hadn't had executives as coaching clients.

5. Giving public talks on applied neuroscience – this journey was less straightforward. I was offered these, but on the premise that I would give them for free. I did a few seminars on that basis and started organising my own workshops. I then used the free seminars to sell tickets to my longer workshops, which worked well. Soon after that, my workshops were noticed by an organisation called Funzing, which offered paid seminars for the general public. My seminars with Funzing turned out to be very popular and generated the biggest share of income for my business at that time.

6. Starting lecturing at university – I had begun to wonder if I could share the same applied neuroscience insights that I'd been covering in my public talks with university students. I really enjoy being in an academic environment and working with students on an ongoing basis to help them deepen their understanding of the brain and its applications in the real world. I started researching where I could do it and was introduced to a professor who in fact had developed and was starting to deliver an MSc in Applied Neuroscience in Organisations. After our Skype chat, he offered me an associate lecturer role on the programme. Lecturing on this online course solidified my feeling that I wanted to share these insights with wider academic audiences, so I started applying for university lecturing positions. I currently lecture at Sheffield Hallam University and feel very

happy to bring my applied neuroscience experience to the academic setting.

In many situations, we need to look at the decision as a sequence of many smaller decisions and allow serendipity to provide us with new options as we go along. Christian Busch, in his book *The Serendipity Mindset* (2020), discusses how this approach is crucial not only for personal but also for corporate solutions. Given that we cannot truly predict the outcome of each decision, we need to adjust as we go along, incorporating PFC rational insights with our mammal-brain-driven gut instincts. Both of these will change as we explore different options, providing us with more information about what next step is most suitable for us. We must be aware that there is a lot of unpredictability in decision-making and we must be prepared to adjust, in both our professional and our personal lives.

Summary of Chapter Six

To summarise, decision-making is a very personal process – although we do like to give advice to people we care about, we are not aware of what would truly make them happy. Often, we are not even rationally aware of what would make us happy either, since emotions are produced by the subconscious centres. Thus, each of us needs to go on an individual decision-making journey to figure out what does and does not work, making some mistakes on the way. As we learn about our preferences and ourselves we make better choices, but there is no shortcut to that. Sometimes we need to be kinder to ourselves when it comes to our mistakes, indecision and the repetition of old patterns that are all part of normal brain functioning. Looking after our brain is also a crucial part of sound decision-making, which we often ignore. Have you ever driven feeling exhausted, started a new relationship when in impossible to soundly judge. Moving past this requires us to break the decision into smaller timelines, make short-term decisions and adjust as we go along. Embracing uncertainty will allow us to be agile and make the best mini-choices in each given situation.

a bad emotional state or had to give a presentation when feeling extremely stressed? Life situations are often not perfect, making it harder to use our best judgement, so we shouldn't beat ourselves up about it too much. As our situation improves, we make more sensible choices. But we can only work with what we have in the given moment – current blood supply, current gut health, current nutrients in the bloodstream, current neurotransmitter balance in the brain, existing brain networks. All these physical components of brain functioning are crucial in determining our psychological and emotional state and rational thinking.

In order to make the best decisions possible we need to note the following points:

1. The appropriate decision-making system should be used for the situation: fast and effortless mammal-brain-driven System I (gut feeling) or methodological and pros-and-cons-based rational PFC-driven System II.

2. When making decisions using System I, be aware of your unconscious biases – you cannot ever truly overcome them, but you can use rational questioning to challenge them.

3. When making decisions in a purely rational System II approach, we might get stuck if there are too many options to choose from (analysis paralysis) or if there are too many variables to consider (like making career choices).

4. We need input from the emotional amygdala and the rational PFC to get unstuck from indecision, make even rational decisions quicker and include other people's needs in our judgements.

5. Some decisions are complex due to lots of unknowns, especially if we are trying to imagine a situation we have never been in before. We can only make decisions based on the information we have and the experiences we can relate to from the past, making completely unfamiliar scenarios

PART III

Changing Relationships

CHAPTER SEVEN

Changing Your Leadership

In this chapter, you will learn:

- What it takes to be an inspiring (resonant) leader at work and in life.
- Why we focus on the task above all else (dissonant leadership).
- Why we revert to dissonant leadership during times of stress, and practical tips on how to manage a stress response.
- How our actions and emotions affect other people.
- What is needed for us to be the best influence on other people.

We all affect other people each and every day: we chat to colleagues at work, interact with our partners and family at home. In each of these interactions we can either be *dissonant* – focused on what tasks need to be achieved and seeing how other people can fit in with that; or *resonant* – empathising and trying to truly understand other people's needs and their points of view. To act in dissonant or resonant ways we activate different networks in our brains. A resonant style is created when we activate a so-called *default mode network* (DMN). This network is responsible for understanding other people, being aware of our own emotions and recognising them in others. This network is also crucial for mentalising, which is understanding other people's ways of thinking. All these great qualities make the DMN crucial for building genuine and trusting relationships. A dissonant style is created when we activate the so-called *task-positive network* (TPN) in the brain. This network is responsible for analytical thinking, prioritising tasks, filtering out distractions, and mathematical reasoning, so it is crucial for getting things done, but can prevent us from truly connecting with others.

Let me provide a couple of examples to illustrate this. Imagine you come home and your partner is very upset. You sit down near them and ask them what is wrong. As your partner talks, you listen patiently, empathising with the situation, with a clear focus on truly understanding the cause behind these feelings and what it is that he or she needs most now. In this situation, you have used a resonant style and have activated the DMN in your brain. Now imagine that instead of doing that your focus is on what you want them to do and you start giving them advice without trying to understand the root causes of their upset. Or maybe you just focus on the fact that you need to book your flights and pretend that you are listening while you are actually searching for the best flights on your phone. In these examples, you will be exhibiting dissonant style and activating the TPN.

Moreover, these styles are contagious: whether we act in a resonant or dissonant way, we bring out the same style in the other person both at the level of their behaviour and their brain activity. When we are being resonant, we activate the DMN in another person, making them more empathic, able to understand and soothe their own emotions, more trusting and genuinely happier. When we are being dissonant, we activate the TPN in another person, making them more closed off, focused on their own thoughts and incapable of truly understanding others and empathising with their state of mind. Moreover, the dissonant style can often trigger a stress response and create negative emotions, with the result that we often want to avoid people who are being dissonant.

Both styles are needed for different reasons: dissonant, to get our tasks done, and resonant, to build social and emotional bonds with others and empower them. This chapter discusses both the neuroscience findings and our behaviour when we are in dissonant and resonant modes and provides some practical tips on how to know which style to choose. We will also look at how stress affects our leadership styles and create a brain-insight-based list of practical ways to manage stress.

Dissonant and resonant leadership

Can you think of a leader who has truly inspired you? It can be somebody from your personal or professional life. Now think what qualities this person possessed. What made them a particularly empowering presence in your life? Write these qualities down. You might come up with some of the characteristics of *resonant leadership*:

- *People-oriented* – this person is really pleasant to be around. Resonant leaders know how to connect with people and understand them.
- *Deeply caring* – this person really cares about you and wishes you to achieve your dreams.
- *Wanting to understand* – you feel visible to this person as they show a desire to understand your thinking and emotions.
- *Aware of others* – this person is constantly aware of the needs and emotional states of others, being able to be there for them if needed.
- *Self-aware* – this leader doesn't see herself/himself as a superior being. Resonant leaders are aware of their own talents, achievements, mistakes and shortcomings, enabling them to relate to whatever you are going through.

- *Mindful* – this leader is comfortable being in the here and now. Resonant leaders pay attention to what is happening around and are fully present in conversations.
- *Compassionate and empathic* – this person accepts others more than just as a means to execute a task. Resonant leaders understand the emotions you feel and can relate to them from their personal experiences. Moreover, this person cares about your feelings and is emotionally present to help you meet your needs. They reassure you if you are scared and encourage you if you don't believe in yourself enough.
- *Trusting* – this person trusts in your abilities, talents and resourcefulness. Resonant leaders don't tell you the answer to each problem but encourage you to find your own solution.
- *Trustworthy and fair* – this person is consistent in her/his behaviour. Resonant leaders are honest and truthful and do not play manipulative games to get people to do what they want. They treat people according to the situation and seek fairness in their teams.

Now let's think about a different person – someone from your personal or professional life who brought the worst out in you. Someone who made you feel small, incapable, unaccepted for who you are. You may come up with a list that includes some of the characteristics of a *dissonant leader* listed below:

- *Task-oriented* – this person mainly cares about the task at hand. Dissonant leaders are so focused on this task that all the other things, such as your needs and fulfilment, are secondary to that. They are not interested in small talk or getting to know you – that would just waste their precious time. Even in a personal setting, dissonant parents and spouses are preoccupied with achieving goals, and are not present emotionally.

- *Achievement-focused* – dissonant leaders mainly care about your achievements and what you can deliver. They aren't interested in how you feel about a task or why you can or can't do something – you are treated based on how well you perform according to their judgement. Dissonant parents reward and praise their kids for good grades and make a big deal if the grades don't their match potential.

- *Self-centred* – this person is wrapped up in her/his own world, believing that she/he knows the best solution to the problem. Therefore, dissonant leaders aren't interested in your approach and aren't open to discussion about it. There is often an air of self-importance and arrogance in dissonant leaders.

- *Authoritative and micromanaging* – their level of self-centredness leads to imposing their views and ideas on what they think is the best solution. They often don't trust others to be capable enough to execute it well, making it hard to delegate. If they give you a task, they might check on your progress and be rather critical of any deviations from their instructions.

- *Stressed and stressing others* – in trying to solve everything and control everyone, this person often experiences huge amounts of stress. Moreover, dissonant leaders stress others out with their approach, leading to agitated teams. In parenting, friendships or romantic relationships this results in feeling as if you are always walking on eggshells and can't truly relax around them.

- *Suffering from mental fatigue and burnout* – due to high levels of stress, dissonant leaders often experience clouded thinking, emotional reactivity and a short temper that can eventually lead to full-blown burnout. Needless to say, people around them often experience mental fatigue, the inability to sleep or relax, and exhaustion.

Now let's look at what happens in the brains of these different leaders, and we will later address what happens in our brains when we are around them too.

Task-positive and default mode networks

The brain consists of millions of brain networks with each dedicated to a distinct function. Dissonant and resonant leaders activate different networks in their brains. Dissonant leaders primarily activate the *task-positive network* while resonant leadership relies on the *default mode network*. Both of these networks are important for normal brain functioning and enable us to do different things.

The task-positive network is crucial to the following functions:

- *Analytical tasks* – this network allows us to analytically assess all the information we have in order to make rationally sound judgements.
- *Execution of well-defined tasks* – imagine we have to create computer code or do some accounting. The rules are very clear and well defined, so this network allows us to execute the task competently and in a timely manner.
- *Focused attention* – the TPN enables us to block out distractions and focus on what needs to be done, so this network is extremely important for staying productive in a noisy office. It also allows us to temporarily forget our personal issues to focus on our work, helping us to meet tight deadlines even if we don't feel great.
- *Working memory* – another crucial component for productivity. The TPN enables us to keep all the information relevant to the task at hand, ensuring speedy execution.

- *Language* – the TPN is needed for us to focus on what it is that we want to communicate to others and helps us stay on track even if people are trying to deviate from the conversation.
- *Logical and causal reasoning* – this network allows us to see a hidden order in things, understand the patterns and see the reasons behind them.
- *Problem-solving* – rationally understanding the causes of the issue is crucial to finding suitable solutions and executing them without deviation.
- *Planning and strategic thinking* – the TPN allows us to plan our day, map out the timeline for the project, think through the possible solutions and critically assess them against each other.
- *Financial assessment and other numerical tasks* – the TPN allows us to understand the rationale between the figures and make sensible choices about budgeting and invest-ment. This network does not take other people's needs into account though, just what would make most sense rationally.

As you can see, when we activate the TPN we are great at getting things done but function rather robotically in terms of our relationships with other people. This network is not capable of empathy, compassion, or understanding our own and other people's emotions. For that, we have the default mode network, primarily activated by resonant leaders.

The default mode network is important for the following functions:

- *Understanding social situations* – it is crucial for getting insights into the social dynamics and reading people's emotions and needs.

- *Understanding and managing emotions* – this network allows us to be in touch with how we are feeling in the situation and enables us to calm the emotions down.
- *Theory of mind* – the DMN enables us to understand the emotional and mental states of others. In that way, we can put ourselves in the shoes of others and see their perspective and experience of the situation. This is crucial for effective communication and resolving conflict, as we will see in Chapter Nine.
- *Moral judgement* – this network enables us to step out of rational pros and cons thinking and take other people's needs and feelings into account.
- *Recalling our past* – activating this network allows us to relate to situations others are experiencing as we are more aware of how we have felt in a similar situation in the past. It is an important quality for compassion and seeing others at the same level as ourselves.
- *Imagining future events* – this network is needed for brainstorming, creativity, planning compelling futures and finding hope in difficult times.

As you can see, the qualities of the DMN complement those of the TPN, allowing us to be well-balanced human beings, focused on getting things done when needed, feeling empathy and being capable of deeply connecting with others. The good news is that we all have a TPN and a DMN! Moreover, we keep on switching between these two networks all the time. The only issue is that the DMN and TPN are opposing networks – they suppress each other, therefore making it physically impossible for us to be rationally calculated and emotionally genuine in our relationships at the same time. Issues occur when we mix up when to use these networks. On the one hand, being stuck in the TPN in a social setting can make us feel isolated and incapable of truly connecting.

Also, in the dissonant state we usually bore the hell out of people as we talk in monologues and don't gauge the interests of other people well. On the other hand, connecting and being driven by empathy in team meetings might not result in achieving a constructive set of objectives. We are also much more distractible and deviate from our original agenda in the resonant mode. The more we practise with one of these networks, the easier it is for us to access it, so it becomes second nature or even a big part of our personality. The key for the majority of people is to train both networks well enough and gain an awareness of when each of them is most appropriate. So how can we do that?

Can we change this behaviour?

The first step is to write down examples of when you are being resonant (activating the DMN) and when you are being dissonant (activating the TPN). Then, next to each, draw a '+' if that produced desired outcomes and a '−' if it was not well received. Some people will be able to come up with a much longer list of one style as opposed to the other – that just shows your personal leadership preference. Now count how many '+'s you have in each style. This will tell you if you managed to make a sound choice on which leadership style to use in the situation. If you find that you tend to be dissonant too often, practise the resonant style by having more conversations where you just listen and try to relate to what the other person is saying. If you notice that you are too social and cannot get things done in a timely manner, try sticking to the dissonant mode where that is needed. The list could look something like this:

- + DMN – chatting to my mum on the phone. It was a suitable network to use as it helped us to connect and be there for each other.

- – TPN – paying my taxes and being fully focused on it while Emilija was desperately trying to get my attention. Looking back, I should have done that task when I wasn't looking after Emilija as I wasn't able to entertain her and was getting irritated by her disturbing me. Next time I will do these types of tasks during her nap or when Emilija is being looked after by others.
- – DMN – during a Zoom meeting with my colleagues. Although it did allow us to connect, I didn't manage to ask the questions I needed answers to, so it would have been useful to have started with the DMN to build rapport and then switch to the TPN to get things done.
- + TPN – writing this chapter. I could hear neighbours chatting in their garden and I had a craving for coffee halfway through, but the TPN allowed me to stay focused on the task, keep in mind the information I wanted to convey and use language to explain it in a logically sound manner.

Brains of team members under different leadership

Resonant leaders are not only fun to be around, but usually they manage to bring out the best in people. In their study, Tony Jack and Richard Boyatzis (Boyatzis et al., 2014) demonstrated that the brains of people recalling experiences with resonant leaders show more DMN activation in their own brains too. In other words, resonant leaders make others more capable of being resonant as well. Moreover, resonant people activate brain centres related to positive emotions, making us feel happy by being around them or just thinking about them. In another study Boyatzis and Jack (Jack et al., 2013) showed that the resonant style of coaching and mentoring also triggers our brain networks responsible for approach behaviours, creating a desire to be around them and reach out to them when needed. Last but not least, we are much more likely to agree with the statements of resonant mentors and be willing do the tasks they ask us to.

In contrast, dissonant leaders trigger other people to become more dissonant as well. People recalling experiences with dissonant leaders in brain scanners activated the TPN, making them much more focused on the task at hand and less capable of being present in social interactions (Boyatzis et al., 2014). Dissonant behaviours also activate other people's brain centres responsible for unpleasant emotions, such as fear, anxiety and worry. That contributes to avoidance behaviours – we rarely want to be around dissonant people and tend not to reach out to them as often. Last but not least, participants were less likely to agree with statements made by experimenters who used dissonant style of mentoring and were reluctant to obey their instructions (Jack et al., 2013).

Why the dissonant approach is not all bad

So which of these leadership styles is more beneficial? It depends. If the situation requires analytical thinking, tight deadlines and laser-like focus on the task, dissonant leaders will help team members stay in the TPN mode needed for it. Resonant leaders in that case would be too distracting as they would supress the TPN so team members would easily lose focus and make more mistakes. Alternatively, resonant leadership is beneficial for those in people-facing jobs (such as managers, teachers, shop assistants, sales representatives), encouraging people to work as a team, and helping the team to make joint decisions, be creative and imagine a brighter future. Overall, resonant leadership often results in higher job satisfaction, more engagement in a team, lower levels of stress and, often, higher performance (remember that positive emotions and lower levels of stress contribute to a higher functioning PFC). Dissonant leadership might be needed in a crisis, when starting a company, working with underqualified employees (as they might need to be micromanaged to learn how to do the task) and when focusing on the task for a long time is essential for good performance.

In our personal lives, we need both modes too. The resonant style allows us to be there for our friends and loved ones emotionally, to truly understand their needs, to make joint decisions, and to have a great time together. The dissonant mode is needed when we are focusing on a task which requires undivided attention, such as booking flights, driving a car, doing online banking, or cooking a complicated meal. In terms of parenting (and being a great teacher), we need to use the resonant style to truly understand kids, promote true motivation in them (that requires first understanding their individual values), encourage them to have fun and be playful, and help them to understand their emotions and be adaptable in social settings. Dissonant leadership is sometimes required when we are helping children to focus on a task, such as doing their homework or learning to ride a bike, or when there is time pressure, for example if we need to get them in the car quickly as we are running late.

Leadership styles and stress

Now let's look at your life. Remember a very challenging day at work – perhaps you had a tight deadline or had to work with people you didn't gel with, or you might have had an argument with your team. At home, your spouse, children, other family members, flatmate or a friend are waiting for you. They are hungry for your attention and want to share news about their day. How do you react? If you are like most people, you might be wrapped up in a dissonant mode, unable to be there for others. Dissonant mode is a natural state for our brains when we are stressed or overwhelmed or if we have something important on our minds to resolve. When we're unable to meet the needs of those closest to us, we can easily get into conflict, which will just make the situation worse as that would be another thing to worry about. What does work better is communicating with your loved ones about what is going on ('I would really love to hear all about your day but I just need 15 minutes to relax first as I have had a very stressful day at work') or, even better, having a family habit of giving people transition time. We have had to implement this in our family – if I have been delivering a long workshop or if Matthew has had a long day at work, we allow each other to have dinner first and then catch up afterwards. Having a bit of time to unwind and let the mind reduce the activity in the TPN network often naturally makes us more sociable later, as the DMN easily kicks in. Also, physical replenishment – relaxing your body by siting down or slouching on the sofa for a bit, nourishing your body with food and water, going for a walk outside in nature, exercising and spending time with loved ones – is needed to reduce overthinking and balance out brain activity.

In terms of work, tight deadlines, poorly performing team members and complaints from clients have a strong power in making us dissonant. That is probably the main reason dissonant leadership is so common, especially in industries where delivering results under tight deadlines is the norm. Companies can run as many leadership training programmes as they like, but it won't change a thing unless the organisational culture is altered to create less stress and more safety. Although it is popular to tackle stress with activities such as lunchtime yoga classes and free gym memberships, these really only reduce the effects of stress. For stress triggers to be addressed at the core, people need to feel safe – a never-ending deadline after deadline marathon feels to our brains like being constantly chased by predators, and resonant leadership cannot happen in that setting. Also, as we discussed before, chronic stress affects the morphology of neurons and reduces the birth of new neurons, making our thinking less adaptable. Interestingly, having safe and consistent relationships can help us to deal with that. Safety induces the release of oxytocin in the brain, which protects neurons from the negative effects of stress hormones, creating resilience, flexibility and the ability to deliver good work. So it is even more important that we have resonant leaders, who care about the needs of their team, make them feel safe and valued, help them to see beyond the current stressful times and provide support and encouragement in a compassionate way when needed. The fair treatment of employees is also crucial for reducing levels of stress and in general creating a place where people have a sense of control over their performance and career progression. Zero-hour and fixed-term contracts, a culture of replaceability, feeling invisible and having no valuable supervision from your line manager create the opposite.

Practical tips to build more resonance

Small things that can make a difference include regular meetings to understand your team members, offering coaching support for staff where they can gain clarity and troubleshoot productivity habits, encouraging teams to connect with meaningful social activities and, first and foremost, truly caring about your team members and treating them fairly. Coaching is actually a great method for that kind of leadership. I remember the jaw-dropping moment eight years ago when I read a chapter on coaching as a leadership style in *Coaching for Performance* by John Whitmore (2009). He suggested using open questions to help team members figure out solutions. In that way, people feel more engaged, valued, trusted and much more committed to the outcome. The leader can train their DMN and truly get to know their team members. Also, that breeds more resonance in the team, helping them to make better joint decisions and have more resilience to stressful situations due to oxytocin (creating a feeling of safety, bonding and trust). John Whitmore created the very practical and useful GROW model, which can be used with teams, family members, or even in self-coaching. Let me briefly guide you through it:

- G stands for Goal – what is it that you are trying to create? Where are you heading? We want to get clear of the destination before we get carried away with the issues of reality. G can be anything – creating a presentation for a client in seven days, losing 10 lbs in a month, earning £4,000 a month, finishing writing the first draft of a book by a specific date.
- R stands for Reality – what is your current situation? How much of the project have you already completed? Have you done this task before? How much weight have you lost recently? How much money are you currently earning? How many chapters are still left to do?
- O stands for Options – what are the ways to achieve it? Let's choose earning £4,000 a month – what are all the ways you could potentially do that? For example, doing twice as many consultation sessions, approaching new companies, selling your car, investing your savings and so on. If you are self-coaching, think about as many options as possible, even the ones that feel impossible. If you are coaching somebody else, just keep asking 'What else?' until they have exhausted their imagination.
- W stands for Willingness – out of all the options you have just brainstormed, we need to weigh them against each other to choose one that you would be willing to do. If the task is large, it's best to choose a small first step towards it that can be completed the same or the next day. For the goals mentioned above, it could be working on a presentation for two 25-minute intervals first thing the following morning; going for a 30-minute walk after work; sending an email to a client you have worked with in the past; writing for 45 minutes first thing in the morning the next day.

This can be a very exciting method to become more resonant with colleagues, friends, family members (and even yourself) – getting to know the real inner workings of another person's mind and helping them to find their own solutions rather than micromanaging, controlling or being emotionally absent.

Mirror neuron system and emotional contagion

Another topic crucial for understanding how we influence and affect each other is emotional and social contagion. Each of us has a so-called mirror neuron system (MNS) in our brain, which make us subconsciously copy the actions of other people. Originally this system was discovered by Dr Giacomo Rizzolatti (Rizzolatti & Craighero, 2004) in studies of the motor cortex in monkeys where neural activity was recorded when they were picking up peanuts to put in a cup. To the astonishment of neuroscientists, the same neurons were also active when monkeys watched the researcher performing the same task – so this neuronal system both allowed monkeys to perform a physical task and kept them in tune with the actions of others, hence the name mirror neuron system. In humans, the MNS is activated when we watch other people play tennis, swim, walk or when we close our eyes and imagine ourselves (or somebody else) doing these actions. Just by watching sports or visualising ourselves doing them, we can potentially improve our performance, as this network will get stronger the more we use it. That is also the way we learn as children – watching others doing things and trying to copy them. In adulthood, we are more susceptible to subconsciously copying people we have a good rapport with. To support that, in the aforementioned research by Tony Jack and Richard Boyatzis (Boyatzis et al., 2014; Jack et al., 2013), the brain scans of people thinking about resonant leaders revealed an increase in activity in the MNS, making them more susceptible to adapting their ways of being and acting. In contrast, remembering experiences with dissonant leaders achieved the opposite – reduced the activity in the MNS, creating a barrier to subconsciously copying their actions.

Similar rules apply with emotions – it's not clear yet if the MNS is involved in empathy, although it has been largely speculated that this is the case. Being in a resonant mode, we are more likely to truly connect with others at an emotional level both by our emotions affecting others and by their emotions influencing us. There seems to be an individual variation though, with some people scoring very high on the empathy scale, and others scoring very low. But all of us are much more empathic when we are being resonant (or activating the DMN) than when we are being dissonant (or activating the TPN). I can't stress that enough – no matter how good our intentions are, if we are stuck in the TPN due to a task-preoccupied mind, we can't truly care about others; it is just physically impossible. So this is yet another reason to practise switching between the TPN and the DMN according to the context of the situation, so we can be there for others when necessary and can get tasks done when we have to. The more we switch between these modes, the quicker and easier switching becomes (again, brain plasticity). The longer we spend in the TPN, the more dissonant we get over time, making it harder and harder to switch into the DMN even in social situations. The same applies with the DMN, of course – the longer we linger in it, the harder it is for us to do tasks in an uninterrupted manner, so performance and productivity on analytical tasks where attention to detail is required might suffer.

Summary of Chapter Seven

We are all leaders in the sense that our actions and emotions have an influence on other people. We do that consciously but also subconsciously. If leadership is the area of your life you feel happy with, it means you have developed pretty healthy interaction habits and can both have meaningful relationships and manage to switch into dissonant mode to get things done. If you struggle to deeply connect with people or in general don't seem to understand the motives behind the actions of others, you probably need to develop your DMN, allowing you to build more resonance. In that way, you will also be more in tune with the actions and emotions of others due to increased activity in your TPN. The odds are that we will have a similar effect on them, helping them to feel more empathy and understanding towards our behaviours. This is particularly useful for people who have been in analytical jobs (such as researcher, data analyst, programmer, accountant) and perfected the activity of their TPN. In some of these career areas, promotion means managing people, and that's when clients often email me as they feel out of their depth when trying to understand and lead a group of people. That transition often takes time, as it requires a new skillset, developing a DMN network to deal with social situations and choosing the resonant style when appropriate. A number of my clients have shared that it feels scary as they have been experts of their field and dealt with things they had more or less 100 per cent control over. Staying dissonant feels familiar and very tempting as you remain an expert directing the actions of others. Stepping into resonant leadership can feel a bit foreign and vulnerable. Also, it does require honest care and a desire to help people. Our brains can easily spot if somebody is putting on an act to get benefits or to manipulate the situation. That won't create resonant leadership, for sure. Often, I ask my clients to get to know people they work with. 'Tell me about the people you manage,' I often ask. Some clients might look puzzled, as they are too busy thinking about the tasks that need to be done or trying to look intelligent enough for their employees, whom they have previously not got to know.

The same applies in personal relationships with romantic partners, family members, friends, kids. We all want to be loved and accepted for who we are, so resonant relationships offer a way of getting to know people on a deeper level. Dissonant relationships often feel absent, as if you are being spoken down to and you feel invisible to the other person. The trickiest thing to manage with leadership is stress, as each of us gets naturally pushed into a dissonant mode under tight deadlines, financial pressures, being overstretched, managing work and family life, mental illness and addiction. Stress-reduction activities, such as good sleep habits, regular breaks and suitable nutrition, all play an important part (as discussed in Chapter Five), but it is most important to deal with the cause of stress. Sometimes this is obvious (such as I don't have the money to pay my rent at the end of the month, my wife has left me) but at other times it is caused by subtle imperfections in multiple areas that add up and might need some deeper work to uncover.

To be the most empowering leaders we need to consider the following points:

1. It's important to recognise which leadership style we tend to fall into under different circumstances and assess if that is the most suitable style.

2. The DMN and the TPN suppress each other, so we need to separate the analytical tasks from the social tasks so that we can best perform in both.

3. We must assess the needs of people we influence with these styles – do they need to focus on the task (requiring the TPN) or does the situation require empathy and social connection (needing the DMN)?

4. Stress and tiredness naturally make us dissonant, therefore regular stress-reduction and replenishment activities are required to stay resonant.

5. We are connected to each other by the mirror neuron system, which enables us to understand the emotional and mental states of others. Therefore, our emotions and actions are contagious.

CHAPTER EIGHT

Changing Your Relationships

In this chapter, you will learn:

- Why we develop certain relationship dynamics and what we can do about it.
- Why we are attracted to people who are not good for us and how we can change that.
- What happens in our brains when we fall in love and why that stage can't last forever.
- Why we start eventually getting annoyed with each other and how we can change that.
- What is needed to create a partnership capable of lasting love and true friendship.

In this chapter, we will look at the importance of relationships and the impact they have on our brains. Many of us will have experienced that warm glow of first falling in love or the great feeling we get when we are in the presence of caring friends or even a colleague with whom we have a great rapport. These feelings are created by a chemical called oxytocin. Oxytocin not only makes us feel great but also increases brain plasticity, protects the brain from the negative effects of chronic stress and helps the brain to function well. By contrast, unpredictable, argumentative and otherwise stressful relationships (called adversarial relationships) do quite the opposite: they reduce brain plasticity, block our creativity, reduce empathy and contaminate our lives with chronic stress.

However, creating empowering relationships is not always easy. Each of us has a completely different brain, which affects our thinking and communication and means we react differently to the same events. Problems occur when we try to understand other people's behaviour using only our own brains, subconsciously making assumptions that they are the same as we are, which leads to a line of misunderstandings. Often, even if we understand that we are different from another person, we still feel lost and misunderstood, which affects our own wellbeing and the dynamics of the relationship. Moreover, there are significant differences in our brains during the different stages of a relationship, which complicates matters even further. In this chapter, we will look at what happens in the different stages of relationships and what components are crucial to creating a true partnership and lasting love.

Attachment styles and the dynamics of relationships

From the moment we are born, we can't help but be influenced by our relationships. The primary relationships we form are with our parents and other caregivers. Based on the dynamics of relationships that our parents and caregivers are capable of, we develop different kinds of attachment, which affect our behaviour, personality traits and relationships in the future.

- *Secure attachment* can form when parents are not only physically but also emotionally present for a child. That allows them to notice the needs of a child and meet them effectively. Moreover, parents set clear boundaries and their behaviour is consistent. When a child is upset, this state is validated and soothed ('Are you scared of the cat? I know some animals can feel scary, but let's try to get to know this cat and it might turn out to be a friendly one'). The amygdala of the child learns that the world is a safe place and that the child is loved and accepted for who they are. Moreover, a child's efforts are being noticed, encouraged and celebrated ('You are trying to climb the steps all by yourself. Such a brave girl'). If required, parents offer constructive support. In other words, the child forms a positive image of their parents and himself/herself. That allows the development of independence, confidence, healthy boundaries with others, and being at ease with appropriate emotional intimacy and closeness.

- *Dismissing/Avoidant attachment* happens when caregivers are emotionally absent from a child, with the child needing to learn self-soothing and self-reliance from a very young age. Often absence is created by valid reasons, including challenging work, business trips, addictions, depression, a large family, the illness of a family member and so on. A child develops a sense that there is nobody truly there for him/her when he/she needs them. That leads to a long-lasting feeling that the child needs to be self-reliant (even when there is no need for it anymore), distant and emotionally unavailable in relationships.

- *Preoccupied/Anxious attachment* is often a result of genetic predisposition (temperament) and inconsistent or irre-sponsive parenting. If the child receives mixed messages, it creates confusion, lack of safety and clinginess to a caregiver. These children get overly invested in their relationships in the future, and their self-worth relies on the approval of others. People with this style of attachment need lots of reassurance and positive encouragement so that they thrive and can build safety in a loving, fully committed and emotionally present relationship with another person who truly cares about that relationship as well.

- *Fearful attachment* results from a sensitive temperament and rejection and criticism from an early age. Adults with this style of attachment seek relationships but are constantly frightened of rejection. As a result, they might end up with overly attached and needy people, whose constant presence and attachment to them can offer safety and reassurance, reducing the fear of rejection, but often leading to co-dependent relationship patterns.

Attachment theory in practice (my story)

In our journey through relationships we can develop different styles of attachment as we heal from childhood trauma. Let me illustrate this with my own story. I grew up in a family of five children who were close in age. My mum had a full-time job as a director and an educator at the preschool day-care. Dad worked full-time as an electrical engineer and competed in chess matches in his spare time. When my older brother and I were toddlers he was a very attentive and fun dad, but that sadly changed when he developed an addiction to alcohol. He became withdrawn from the family and spent most of his time in his workshop, playing chess and drinking. Moreover, we had a small farm of cows, pigs and chickens, grew vegetables and had a large orchard, entirely run by my mum and us five children. Mum was overstretched, working 8 a.m. to 6 p.m., cooking, cleaning and looking after farm animals the rest of the time. She was getting up at 4.30 a.m. each morning and going to bed past 11 p.m. each night. They were arguing about my dad's drinking, how he was not involved in the farm and setting a bad example for us kids, which probably made him drink more.

As one of the oldest children, I looked after my younger sisters when my mum worked at the farm. I felt I had to be strong and protective for both my mum and my sisters, which felt like a big responsibility at a pre-teen age. I developed a pronounced dismissing attachment, becoming very resourceful and self-reliant, and dated rather emotionally unavailable guys during my university years. My biggest dream was to have a happy family with somebody with whom I could have a true partnership. However, this was not possible unless I found a way to heal. My mammal brain was unfortunately drawn to people who created a familiar feeling to the relationship I had known with my father – emotionally unavailable men. That created lots of suffering as I constantly felt unseen and didn't feel my partner was there for me when I was going through rough patches, for example during my PhD. Once I developed strong attachment in a relationship my style would change from dismissing/avoidant to preoccupied/anxious, making me obsessed with the relationship. My amygdala would get a sense of safety when I was with my partner and freak out when we were apart. Needless to say, that led to spending lots of time together, which was great to start with but compromised other areas of my life – friends, exercise, putting more hours into the work I love, turning opportunities down if it meant being away from my partner. I was also clingy, and not able to offer much freedom for my partner, or suffering inside if I did offer that. So I started to look at how I could change the co-dependent dynamics to a more empowering partnership with healthy boundaries.

We need to see things for what they are. We need to understand the root causes of the dynamics in our relationships if we are to heal them. One of the most helpful methods for achieving this is inner child healing from transactional analysis (TA) psychoanalytic theory, developed by Eric Berne (2015).

Healing traumas from childhood and previous relationships

According to TA, each of us possesses three personality states: inner adult (IA), inner child (IC) and inner parent (IP). We get into each of these states depending on the situation and brain activity:

- The *inner adult* state is created by a well-functioning and active PFC. In that state we are rational, objective, and able to assess the current situation in a balanced manner, understanding the needs and emotions of ourselves and another person.
- *Inner child* represents a mammal-brain-dominant state. It is joyful and playful (natural child) until the amygdala gets triggered (adapted child), creating emotional reactivity (jealousy, anger, aggression) or shutdowns.
- The *inner parent* state represents the imprinting of the behaviours and communication styles of our early upbringing. People who experienced a lot of criticism during childhood often have a strong critical inner parent voice, and the ones who were nurtured in a consistent manner usually develop a nurturing inner parent.

The combination of the inner child's wounds and inner parenting style creates our individual trauma behaviours. IC wounds can fall into the categories of abandonment, guilt, trust or neglect, depending on what we have experienced during our childhood and in previous romantic relationships. I relate strongly to abandonment wounds – I feel the happiest in the presence of my partner and my amygdala freaks out when he is away for long periods of time. Rationally that does not make sense – I know he is OK and will be back, there is nothing indicating any risk of him leaving us, but my amygdala doesn't buy it as the mammal brain cannot think rationally. It is unable to assess the situation objectively.

Healing inner child/amygdala desensitisation

To heal my amygdala, I needed to go through these steps:

1. *Retrain the IP:* Use my rational inner adult (PFC) to train up my inner parent (combination of the PFC and mammal brain centres) so it can soothe my abandonment-fearing inner child. My critical inner parent would just tell my inner child off, creating negative mind chatter: 'Don't be ridiculous, there is nothing to worry about', 'You are being unreasonable, stop that'. But that makes the inner child feel even worse and can result in a downward spiral.

2. *Validate the feelings of the IC:* Nurturing messages from the inner parent validate the inner child's subjective experience and offer safety and perspective: 'I know you are scared and feel lonely, but you are not alone. I am here for you and so are many other people who truly care about you. You are beautiful, talented and have so much to offer in your relationship. Your partner truly loves you and demonstrates that every day [insert some evidence here, such as she/he always comes back home to you; chose to marry you/have children with you] in the best way that she/he can given what is going on in her/his life' (that offers perspective and widens IC thinking in a caring and gentle way).

3. *Understand and meet the needs of the IC:* The inner parent can ask the inner child, 'What is it that you need right now? How can I help you to feel better?' In that way, we get to know what needs our mammal brain centres are not meeting at a sufficient level. Is it safety? Significance? Love and connection? Sit with this question and once you realise which of the needs are missing, have a think about how you can help your inner child to meet them. For example, lack of safety could be met by creating nurturing rituals – a hot bath,

other self-care behaviours – or the inner parent explaining to the inner child what is going well in your life right now (such as 'I know you are scared, but we have enough savings and are in a very safe place financially. We are also healthy and have a lovely place to live.') If you haven't done any IC healing before, having internal conversations of that kind will feel very strange so you might feel reluctant to do so. In that case, you might want to read more on IC healing to assess that for yourself (for example, Lapworth & Sills, 2011). I have seen great results using this technique with my coaching clients, and in my personal life. Finding an internal way to soothe your amygdala reduces emotional reactivity, neediness and resentment, allowing you to respond to situations from a PFC-dominant, balanced and objective inner adult perspective.

Past trauma is not easy to change and it requires repetitive and consistent exposure to the opposite to build new networks. Interestingly, brain plasticity is enhanced by oxytocin when we are in a loving and consistent relationship. As an immediate effect, oxytocin creates a feeling of trust and safety, allowing the brain to enter thriving mode. In such a state, we can afford the luxury of learning and changing. The body and brain can relax and switch to the parasympathetic nervous system, creating a good supply of oxygen and nutrients to the neocortex. That increases our repertoire of perspectives and behavioural patterns and allows us to evaluate the situation in a much more objective manner. According to TA, we can function under the inner adult, responding to the current situation rather than past trauma. Even if we have had hurtful or even traumatic relationships in our childhood and/or past relationships, we can build and strengthen new networks, signalling safety to our mammal brain centres. That allows a gradual shift in the attachment style.

In contrast, stressful and unpredictable relationships put our brains into survival mode where we function on amygdala-dominant reactivity. Chronically elevated levels of cortisol in adversarial relationships supress brain plasticity, making it incredibly difficult for us to change our old patterns. Our amygdala-dominant thinking distorts the reality, reducing the options even further. We revert to an adapted inner child state, causing past hurts to surface and amplify our reactivity. The more we engage in these relationships, the stronger these old brain networks become, creating more and more rigid patterns over time. Acting that way, we get rejected, criticised and even abandoned by our partners, accumulating even more trauma for the amygdala (called amygdala over-sensitisation). This downward spiral makes us even more reactive, reinforcing our old hurtful attachment styles. So, to become unstuck in this area we need to be with people who are healthy for us. But time and time again, we seem to be attracted like magnets to what we call the 'wrong people' – why is that? Also, when we meet somebody and feel some 'chemistry' or very strong physical attraction, it requires a tremendous effort not to get involved even when we see big red flags in their behaviour. Why is that and is there anything we can do about it?

Why we choose the wrong people: Imago theory and the romantic stage of relationships

One of the main questions I get asked in my coaching sessions and seminars on relationships is: Why am I attracted to the wrong people? In his book *Getting the Love You Want*, psychotherapist and bestselling author Harville Hendrix (2020) discusses his Imago theory, explaining the root causes of that paradox. According to Hendrix, in childhood we form an attachment to our parents and other caregivers and certain behaviours and traits cause us pain while others give us pleasure. In that way, we create a matrix of familiar traits linked to positive and negative associations. Rationally, we want to avoid all the traits we label as negative, but our mammal brain centres are drawn to familiarity as that gives them a sense of safety. When we grow up, we think we will choose somebody who will support our values and do away with the negative experiences we had as children. When we meet someone who seems to tick all the boxes in our PFC assessment, however, our mammal brain centres are silent – the relationship lacks the sense of familiarity to even be registered. Remember, the mammal brain's input is crucial for creating emotions, so the silent mammal brain won't result in falling in love, physical attraction or a desire to spend time with that person. In contrast, if we meet somebody who has enough familiar traits to our caregivers, the mammal brain is drawn to that person like a mosquito to a light – we don't know why (as the PFC is not aware of mammal brain motifs) but we are besotted with that person. We say things like, 'Wow, it seems as if I have known you for ages', 'We have so many things in common, I can't believe that'. What the mammal brain is really saying is, 'Mum/Dad, we are reunited!'

According to Harville Hendrix (2020), you have met your Imago match – a person who is congruent with the image your mammal brain has built by mixing and matching the traits of your parents and other caregivers. However, the reward centres of the mammal brain – the ventral tegmental area (VTA) – produce dopamine and send it to the nucleus accumbens (NAcc), which causes pleasure when we spend time with that person. Dopamine is very addictive and makes our life all about the person – you can't get enough of them when you are together and can't stop thinking about them when you are apart. Moreover, VTA also has GABA-filled neurons connected to the PFC that inhibit critical thinking, making it impossible to soundly assess if that person is suitable for us. We get more and more involved and invested in the relationship, infatuated with the upsides and blind to the downsides. That is the first stage of a relationship – the *romantic love phase*.

Let's take two partners, Jackie and Tony. They meet at a work party held by Tony's company. Tony, being a responsible and serious guy, subconsciously reminds Jackie of her dad, who was very focused on his work and providing for his family. Although Jackie did not get to spend much time with her dad due to his frequent business trips, she felt loved and cared for. Jackie treasured each Sunday she got to spend with her dad and was secretly competing for his attention with her brother Tim. Tony grew up with flamboyant parents who loved travelling and going to fancy restaurants and always had friends around. Tony was an introverted boy, hated the constant change of frequent travelling, new people, and the varied hobbies his parents pushed him to do. Nonetheless, meeting Jackie, a stunning impeccably dressed and well-travelled lady with various interests, feels exciting and strangely familiar to his mammal brain. They click immediately and start spending lots of time together.

In this romantic phase of their relationship, Jackie and Tony get so involved that they temporarily merge their lives, desires and priorities. They are getting so much reward from the relationship that everything else is pushed down the priority list. This stage is, unfortunately, not designed to last. The reward centres of the brain become desensitised, reducing the amount of dopamine secreted and making us less infatuated with that person. That allows our PFC to kick in and give us more of an objective view of the person. We might start prioritising our work, friends and hobbies, changing the dynamics of the relationship, which can further add to the increasing friction and arguments. As Harville Hendrix (2020) would say, welcome to the *power struggle stage* of a relationship.

What was I thinking when I chose him/her: the power struggle stage of relationships

'Why can't I just be happy in my relationship?' – I often get asked this by my clients. First, this question already highlights the common misunderstanding of what role a romantic relationship actually serves. Clients explain to me that they just want their lives to be nice and easy and their partners to always be supportive. It isn't realistic to expect our partners to always be supportive and never critical. Each of us is a combination of opposites and we see the world through the prism of our individual value hierarchy. So when we choose partners, we often have some overlap in values to create common ground, but other values can be outside our value system.

Being attracted to people with different values

Let's go back to Jackie and Tony. Jackie loves city holidays, nice clothes, jazz concerts and eating out with friends. She works in the city as a management consultant and spends pretty much all she earns, often getting into debt by the end of the month. Tony is dedicated to his IT business – he works really long hours and wants to chill at home with a takeaway or cook a simple meal and watch movies. He is dedicated to saving and wisely investing money. He could retire given his investment portfolio, but he loves his work and wants to build an even greater financial fortune. Jackie spending money on fashionable clothing, expensive concerts and fine dining irritates Tony and he labels Jackie as irresponsible. Jackie is starting to find Tony's life boring and feels gutted that they can't spend lots of time together travelling to different cities, exploring new restaurants and enjoying the world's best jazz musicians. Which of them is in the right? Of course, that is a silly question and we will take the side of the one whose values are closer to our own.

Our childhood experiences might influence our values and interpretations of other people's actions as well. If we had parents who were very frugal and their dedication to saving money caused us pain (like not being able to go skiing or having to wear cheap clothes while other kids had fashion labels), we would tend to rebel against that behaviour. Alternatively, if we have been indoctrinated by authority and parental figures about the importance of saving, we might label Tony as the responsible one and Jackie as immature. If we had parents who were careless with money we might be likely to seek financial safety as adults. But if we had great memories of our parents splashing out on anything we needed and having a luxurious life, that might appeal to us as well, pushing us into Jackie's type of lifestyle.

All these experiences add up and trigger our reward or pain centres. We tend to seek behaviours that we associate with pleasure and try to avoid the ones that bring memories of pain. Interestingly, though, we are likely to get together with somebody whose values challenge us (like Tony and Jackie), creating a need to expand and grow. In the romantic phase of their relationship, Tony doesn't care so much about his work and is happy to put jobs on hold to spend time with Jackie. He is willing to explore jazz venues and go out for expensive dinners and is thrilled to hear Jackie's stories from her travelling days. Jackie is impressed by Tony's stable and kind personality – she feels safe around him and admires his dedication to work.

When the values of partners start to clash

After the romantic phase has ended, the second stage – the power struggle – begins. Tony is busy catching up with work and doesn't give as much attention to Jackie as before. Jackie feels lonely and is longing for the attentiveness Tony used to show. Moreover, the traits that they once admired in each other start to bother them. When we meet, of course, differences in behaviour offer excitement and novelty. Living together for a while, these differences start to clash with and compromise our own values. Jackie's extravagant and expensive lifestyle is challenging Tony's desire to accumulate wealth. Tony's dedication to work is taking travelling opportunities away from Jackie, as she does not want to spend lots of time apart. They start feeling resentful and argue more and more.

Aligning values and creating conscious partnerships

To reach the third stage, the *conscious partnership phase*, we need to fully accept the other person for who they are and learn to communicate and collaborate with them effectively. To reach acceptance and change their perspectives, Tony needs to link his values to Jackie's and vice versa. This step-by-step process developed by Dr John Demartini (2007) can help them do that:

1. Tony needs to identify his top three values using Demartini's value questionnaire we covered in Chapter Three. Tony comes up with: 1) Work; 2) Finances; 3) Relationship with Jackie.

2. Jackie needs to do the same questionnaire to determine her top three values, which are: 1) Romantic relationship; 2) Exciting experiences: travelling, fine dining, jazz concerts; 3) Aesthetic beauty: nice clothing, interior design.

3. Tony needs to link Jackie's top three values to his top three values to work out how specifically the things that Jackie cares about are serving things that he cares about. The list could look something like this (I will name seven links, but would suggest expanding the list to 20, 30, or even 50 if possible, in order to build well-formed positive associations linking different value systems):

- Jackie's dedication to our relationship makes her always available to spend time together and adjust to my work schedule.
- Jackie encouraging me to travel can build business opportunities abroad.
- Jackie is so good-looking and skilful at choosing nice outfits. I can learn a lot from her about how I could look more representative to my business partners.
- Jackie's desire to explore new activities can expand my horizons for new business ideas, creating more financial adaptability in the long term.
- Jackie's desire to spend lots of time together encourages me to spend more time away from work, helping my PFC to replenish and function better the next day.
- Going to high-quality music events, fine dining and just spending a pleasant time with Jackie causes the release of dopamine, serotonin and oxytocin in my brain, creating more blood flow to my neocortex. That in turn makes me sharper and more creative.
- In spending more time with Jackie, I am training my DMN which allows me to be a more resonant leader at work with my employees and connect at a deeper level with my clients.

4. Jackie needs to link Tony's value hierarchy to her own, as Tony did for hers in the previous step. We need to try to be as creative and open-minded as possible when doing this exercise, so being in a relatively calm and well-rested state is advisable. If you feel very resentful towards your partner or hurt by their actions, you might need to go for a walk or do a breathing exercise first.

This exercise should help to reduce friction between differences in value hierarchy. If one of the partners is feeling inferior to the other, you could extend the exercise to linking your values to another person's – how specifically are the things that you care about serving another person? That would help to level out the balance of the relationship. If there is lots of past hurt being triggered by the dynamics, it is also important to soothe the amygdala with IC healing techniques, as discussed earlier. In the next chapter, we will discuss what is needed for Tony and Jackie to start communicating more effectively, so they feel heard, respected and can reach compromises. But before that, let's look at the seven principles of successful relationships developed by researcher and bestselling author Dr John Gottman (2018) from his 20 years of studying relationships.

Cultivating a true friendship

Dr John Gottman was fascinated and puzzled by what makes a successful and lasting relationship. Seeing divorce rates skyrocket within the last 50 years in the US and worldwide, despite a boom in marriage counselling, he decided to try to truly understand why some couples succeeded while others failed. To achieve that, he set up his Apartment Lab (also called the Love Lab) where couples would spend 24 hours doing their usual things while being filmed and their stress levels monitored (measuring heart rate and cortisol levels in the urine). It does sound pretty awkward to spend a weekend with your partner that way, but most couples soon eased into it and were having a usual leisurely time and also discussing unfinished disagreements. I will share insights into what makes communication constructive and styles that are destructive for relationships in the next chapter. For now, we will look at the seven core principles for building a solid and lasting relationship.

Each couple that Gottman labelled as 'masters' were very skilled at these seven steps and did them either naturally or put a conscious effort into remembering to do them. The couples who were labelled as 'disasters' scored very low at each step, and often didn't even see the point of them. The following tips will work for those couples who are somewhere in the middle, between 'masters' and 'disasters', and still have a desire to be together, but feel that they are gradually growing apart. The first three principles deal with strengthening friendship, the next three tackle dealing with conflict and the last one addresses the highest level of connection – creating shared meaning.

1. *Enhancing your love maps (keep getting to know your partner).* We can't feel safe, significant or connected in the relationship if we feel invisible. Therefore, an enjoyable and lasting partnership requires truly getting to know each other and updating our inner map of the other person regularly. In doing so, we also reinforce the idea that the other person thinks and experiences situations differently from us. Also, discussing important events and our perceptions of them will reduce mind-reading and second-guessing and ultimately lead to better understanding, emotional connection and more intimacy. We start with asking the other person open-ended questions, such as, 'What activity do you enjoy most?' 'What are the stressors that you experience at work?' 'What is your biggest fear?' 'What aspects of parenting do you enjoy most?' 'What aspirations do you have for the next five years?' These questions seem obvious and we might be reluctant to ask them either because we feel we know the answers or we fear our partner might expect us to know. But in reality, we can't know, we have different brains and can only second-guess based on our own way of thinking. Getting to know the real answers will give

you more knowledge about the inner mechanisms of that person and your partner will feel more visible to you. It is important also that you share quality information about your inner world as well, such as deep desires, fears, dreams, past experiences, current challenges and joys. We are not designed to mind-read and if you do feel resentful towards your partner for not knowing these important things about you, you are also partly to blame. 'Sharing is caring' is a phrase we're all familiar with and that definitely applies to couples. Asking quality questions and sharing important information with each other will lead to a stronger lasting friendship and partnership.

2. *Nurture your fondness and admiration.* You cannot have a true and lasting love for anyone you do not like and respect. You can have the romantic stage of love, which is mainly based on physical attraction, but that will fade away. Lasting love and friendship require accepting and embracing the other person for who they are. Linking the other person's way of being to your top three values might help you to see some of the differences in a more positive way. Another way to reignite fondness and admiration in long-term relationships is recalling the beginning of the relationship and sharing these stories – How did you meet? What was it that attracted you to each other? What was the best holiday you had? What talents does your partner have? What are their top three values that they are truly dedicated to? With time, the amount of unresolved conflict and resentment accumulates and we often develop nega-tive bias towards another person. The amygdala is mostly interested in what the other person did wrong and totally ignores all the amazing things they do. So, starting to pay attention to the situations where the other person truly showed up and thinking about how their values link to your

values would counterbalance amygdala bias, allowing you to build a more objective view of who that person is. Don't just stop there – share with your partner what things you appreciate or admire about them. They can be current, or from the past. Start developing the habit of sharing positive things about each other, to create a buffer for harder times.

3. *Turn toward each other instead of away.* When interacting with your partner, attention, effort and time are required for psychological safety, significance and true connection. If we feel offended or just simply too busy, we might close off and be unavailable. It is important in these times to explain what is happening and postpone the interaction to a more suitable time. Sometimes we develop a habit of meeting the need for significance by withdrawing attention or connection to the partner (for example, 'He didn't listen about my day yesterday, so I will ignore what he is saying now'). That can be very harmful for the relationship and incorporating more transparent communication about how we feel in certain situations can make a huge difference: 'I am interested in how your day went. But there is something I need to share with you first. Last night, I was very eager to discuss my day with you and you seemed to be disengaged. I felt sad as our connection and being there for each other is very important to me. Could we discuss what was happening for you that evening so I gain a better understanding of that behaviour?' Honesty and transparency are needed to tackle situations that are tricky. Shutting down, withdrawing or escaping into alternatives might provide temporary relief, but will chip away at the relationship long term. Also, a couple could come up with their own rituals that make them feel visible to each other – holding hands, maintaining eye contact, putting the phone down or pausing the TV when another person

is talking. It might be a good idea to discuss these things explicitly – how do you like best to be listened to? What behaviours make you shut down or feel invisible?

4. *Let your partner influence you.* In long-term relationships, complete independence or complete co-dependence are not sustainable. Successful long-term relationships require both individuals co-creating the dynamics and the decisions of the relationship together. In these so-called interdependent relationship dynamics, both partners accept differences in the way they would personally handle parenting, distribution of household chores, handling money, the living situation and so on. If both partners try to do things 100 per cent their own way that creates an adversarial relationship where constant fighting and tension are inevitable. If one partner gives in totally just to keep peace and to make the other happy, that builds resentment and unmet needs over time. In order to create a situation where everyone's needs are being met, these differences need to be discussed openly and compromises made. That does require seeing your partner at the same level though. If we see ourselves as more entitled or better than another person, we tend to give orders and criticise them into submission, leading to a lack of significance, connection and expression for one partner and a lack of true partnership for both. If we are infatuated with our partner, seeing them as a superior being, we shrink, accept orders and lose self-fulfilment over time. Often, we might alternate between putting our partner on a pedestal and throwing them in the pit. If that is the current dynamic, we need to work on balancing our perception to level out the field.

Dr John Demartini's breakthrough method: In this method, we write down the top five traits we most admire about this person and the top five traits we most despise about them.

Then we challenge these perceptions, asking, 'When and where did this person show the opposite trait?' It might be tricky at the start, especially if we have internal phrases such as 'always' or 'never' near that trait. The reality is we all have all the traits there are, but we just display them in different settings and to a different extent. It is best to do this exercise when you are not feeling actively resentful towards your partner to reduce that bias. Think for as long as it takes to come up with at least five to ten examples where this person displayed the opposite of each trait (both negative and positive traits) to balance that skewed perception. The next step is to see these traits in ourselves – write five to ten examples for each trait where you have displayed these very same traits. It might be in a different area of your life (for example, if you are working on the trait of your partner being critical of you, you might find that you are also critical of him, your kids, your colleagues and yourself). Creating more objective perceptions of our partners and ourselves will naturally put us at the same level, which is crucial in developing interdependent dynamics and making family choices that take everyone's needs into account.

5. *Solve your solvable problems.* We must try to dig deeper and get to the root cause of the conflict – what are the needs that person is trying to meet? Learning to communicate these needs and differences in a non-violent way allows us to better understand the motives of another person, which will be easier than trying to find mutual ground for a solution.

6. *Some problems cannot be solved by reaching a compromise.* They might originate from fundamental differences between people, and if both partners accept these differences and learn to live around them, it can still result in a lasting and happy relationship. If we try to make the partner into somebody we want them to be rather than embracing who

they are, that will result in an endless source of conflict. Exploring how these seemingly unresolvable differences serve us, rather than get in the way, will help us change our perspective. Take Tony being truly dedicated to saving money and working as hard as he can, which triggers feelings of resentment and loneliness in Jackie. If Jackie can gain a clearer picture of how Tony's trait is serving her and their relationship, rather than her focusing on trying to change Tony's ways, this will create much better understanding and appreciation. Also, it's best to avoid 'moral judgements' here, such as 'dedicated husbands do…', 'good fathers should…' That just keeps us stuck in a fantasy where both partners cannot be appreciated for who they truly are.

7. *Creating shared meaning.* In addition to strengthening friendship and ironing out friction due to differences, adding shared meaning to the relationship will help to keep the relationship fresh and exciting and allow us to build special joint experiences. The method of building shared meaning will differ for each couple; some might love to have a shared hobby (such as playing tennis, mountaineering, travelling), others share meaning by successfully co-parenting their children, running joint businesses or renovating their dream house. In day-to-day life, even small joint rituals such as having Sunday morning brunch out in a new café each time, or learning to cook different meals together can make a huge difference. Have a brainstorming session with your partner on what would be an exciting joint venture for both of you and start putting it into action.

These seven principles will form a strong basis for building a lasting relationship and strengthening connection and love over time. In fact, recent independent research studies (Davoodvandi et al., 2018; Garanzini et al., 2017) have confirmed that heterosexual and homosexual couples that followed these seven principles significantly improved their marital adjustment and intimacy. In the next chapter, we will discuss how we can add transparent and honest communication so we can express ourselves clearly and also listen to the other person's needs.

Summary of Chapter Eight

Before we move on, let's summarise what we need to do in order to develop true partnerships:

1. Understand that the type of partners we choose and the dynamics we develop in the relationship are influenced by our early attachment style.
2. Identify our inner child wounds and heal any issues that are getting in the way of us creating an inner adult-based safe, trusting and mutually empowering relationship.
3. Realise that no matter how much we desire to run away from childhood trauma, the mammal brain is drawn to select partners that resemble our caregivers enough to create the familiarity crucial for emotional connection.
4. Accept that the romantic phase of the relationship cannot last forever. Once that phase ends, we are left with the power struggle caused by the friction of mismatching values. To reach the lasting true love stage, we need to develop a true partnership.
5. Remember that a true partnership and lasting love require deep friendship, where we appreciate each other for who we truly are, learning to manage conflict effectively and building shared meaning.

CHAPTER NINE

Changing Your Communication

In this chapter, you will learn:

- The difference between mammal-brain-dominant thinking and human-brain-dominant thinking and what types of conversations we are capable of in these different states.
- The best ways to express ourselves without encountering resistance from others.
- How we can listen to others in a way that means we truly understand them.
- What communication mistakes we should most avoid in relationships and some better alternatives to them.
- The practical tools to tackle our negative inner chat.

Have you ever been offended by something another person said? Perhaps you felt that – without really meaning to – you offended the other person too? What happened next? Both people probably felt misunderstood, perhaps angry or sad. Most problems in romantic and working relationships happen because of misunderstandings in communication.

This is normal. Each of us has a very different brain and we see the world differently. Moreover, our brain has a threat response system (also known as fight, flight or freeze), which is triggered if we feel challenged or detect any real or imaginary danger. In that state, each of us becomes emotionally reactive, irrational and selfish, making good communication nearly impossible. In this chapter, we will look at the different brain states we get into each day (mammal-brain-dominant and human-brain-dominant) and what conversations we are capable of in each of them. Then we will discuss what triggers them and how to manage these states in ourselves. Last but not least, we will cover how to express ourselves without triggering a threat response in another person, so as to have the best chance of being listened to and understood.

Why we get into irrational arguments and how to avoid them

Any form of communication consists of two main components: expressing (talking) and receiving (listening). Both of them are influenced by the way our human, mammal and lizard brain centres function at that given moment. As we have discussed before, the part of the human brain called the PFC is the most capable to truly grasp what is being said, process it and express our take on the matter in a balanced way. This part needs lots of energy and calm emotional mammal brain centres (amygdala, reward centres). If the amygdala is triggered by something that has been said, it temporarily blocks the rational brain centres, resulting in mammal-brain-dominant thinking and emotional reactivity. Let's revisit Dr John Gottman's Apartment Lab (aka the Love Lab). Each couple tested there was asked to discuss neutral events, pleasant events and also something that they had had a disagreement about while being monitored on camera (Gottman & Silver, 1994). One couple, let's call them Daniel and Judy, had a disagreement about getting a dog, so had to discuss their views on that. From just a brief snapshot of how couples discussed their issues, John could predict which of the couples would most likely stay together and which would probably split up eventually (we will get back to that later). As the conversations got heated over controversial topics, couples became less and less considerate towards each other, resulting in higher reactivity, more rage, and all-or-nothing statements (such as 'You always want to get your way'). The experimenters interrupted half of the couples, saying that the microphones were not working, and spent ten minutes pretending to fix them. The couples had to pause their conversations, which were restarted ten minutes later. Interestingly, after the break, couples sounded a lot more rational and were better at attempting to understand their partner's point of view. Increasing activity in the amygdala prior to the break was reducing the activation of the PFC, making it impossible to stay rational, show empathy, consider the other person's needs and suppress unwanted behaviours. The neutral break allowed the amygdala to calm down, giving them a chance to get back to PFC-dominant thinking. It's important to remember that when we are experiencing amygdala hijack, we exhibit good self-awareness, so we don't realise that we are being ridiculous. Trying to make a sound judgement on what to do in that state is futile. We should use our PFC-dominant calm and rational state to come up with an idea of what would be the most feasible way to stop our amygdala from getting carried away. Here are a few ideas to get you started:

- *Find a good time for the conversation* – make sure that neither you nor your partner is in a PFC-depleted state or already feeling anxiety or other amygdala-dominant emotions. If either partner notices that they are getting into the amygdala-hijack state, take a ten-minute break.
- *Use the Pomodoro Technique* – if you both know that you need to have a tricky conversation, it is worth agreeing in advance with your partner to have a break and setting a timer – talk for 20 minutes, with 10 minutes' break, then continue for another 20 minutes afterwards if needed.

- *Choose a calming environment for a conversation* – try going for a walk together, sitting by a pond/river/aquarium or sitting in the garden or on a cosy sofa. It is not a good idea to discuss it while driving or in the morning when you are both rushing to get ready.

- *Do a breathing exercise (as discussed earlier) or meditation before the conversation* – given that it will be tricky to stay sensible enough to remember to do it when the amygdala gets carried away, doing a breathing exercise before the conversation might give you a chance to be more considerate in how you express yourself to start with.

- *Learn each other's mammal-brain-dominant reactions* – while some people get more and more talkative when the amygdala is activated, others tend to shut down and withdraw. Learning to identify each other's signs of amygdala response might help you make a better choice and identify when a break is required.

In addition to these tips, effective communication requires expressing and learning to listen in ways that are amygdala-friendly, which we will discuss in the next section. But first, let me discuss the different kinds of conversations we are capable of based on our thinking and emotional state. As we have learned, if the amygdala has been triggered, it hijacks the PFC, resulting in mammal-brain-dominant thinking. In that state, we either express our emotions in a raw PFC-uncensored manner, producing an active attack, or suppress unwanted emotions, resulting in withdrawal and closing off. During withdrawal, the war continues inside, causing stress, draining energy and further compromising rationing thinking. Neither in an active attack nor in the passive withdrawal state are we capable of being in the present moment, hearing what has been said accurately, understanding another person's point of view, accepting differences in opinions, feeling empathy or caring about consequences. Only when the amygdala is experiencing enough safety can we expect the PFC to be at its best capacity, creating PFC-dominant thinking. That allows us to share our ideas and points of view in a constructive manner and learn about other people's take on it as well (intellectual discussion). In the PFC-dominant state, we can also be emotionally present for ourselves and for others. That allows us to accurately identify how the topics discussed are making us feel and enables us to empathise with the feelings expressed by the other party (honest dialogue).

Honest dialogue is the type of conversation that is required to build a strong connection between people and gain emotional intimacy, and can, if done properly, ultimately lead to the healing of past traumas. If we do experience invalidation or criticism of the things we share, even if well meant ('Oh dear, you have so much in your life. You must be grateful for it, not depressed'), it triggers the amygdala, which pushes us to lash out or withdraw. In general, at the core, we all want to be loved and accepted for who we are, and the amygdala is particularly sensitive to that. Therefore, the techniques we will discuss later have a validation step as a key component to foster emotional safety, trust and connection. Moreover, emotional safety is a crucial component for creating constructive change in the dynamics of a relationship, which we will discuss at the end of the book.

Communication for connection (Imago conversation)

Given the primitive origin of the amygdala, it requires lots of safety. One of the best methods I have come across for amygdala-friendly communication is the Imago dialogue developed by Harville Hendrix and Helen LaKelly Hunt (2017). This method helps you to develop a dialogue, which enables you to communicate your experience, empathise with feelings and learn to accept differences in perception. To keep the flow uninterrupted, people take turns to be a so-called sender (person who talks) and receiver (person who is trying to understand the sender's point of view). To achieve a complete dialogue, we need to go through these stages:

- *Making an appointment* – as discussed earlier, it is crucial to choose an appropriate time for a conversation. Each person needs to make sure that their amygdala is fairly calm and the PFC is well replenished. You might also want to share briefly what the emotional flavour of the conversation is to help another person to assess if they are feeling capable of dealing with it and also to help them prepare for the conversation emotionally. It could sound like this: 'I would like to discuss my work frustrations with you, would now be a good time?' Or, 'I would like to share with you how much I appreciate you. Could we talk about it now or at some point later?' By making an appointment, you show respect for another person's boundaries, which is already an amygdala-friendly approach. In communication, we want to avoid anything that can trigger the amygdala, and interrupting your partner in the middle of their activity can very much do that.

- *Sharing a subjective experience* – in this step the sender shares what they are experiencing with a non-accusatory 'I' statement. It could sound like this: 'I have been feeling saddened and frustrated this morning. I have noticed that you have been checking your phone and did not appear to be listening when I was discussing the concerns I had about my work with you.'

- *Mirroring* – in the mirroring stage, the receiver feeds back exactly what they have heard without adding any of their opinions to it. Receiver: 'Let me see if I am getting this right. You were feeling saddened and frustrated this morning when I didn't appear to be listening to your concerns about your work. Is that accurate?' Sender: 'Yes, you've got it.' Receiver invites them to share more: 'Is there anything else that you would like to share about that?' Sender: 'Well, yes, I really appreciate our relationship, and having the chance to express my worries to you means a lot to me. Having the chance to talk things over with you calms me down and also I appreciate your perspective on the situation.' Receiver: 'Let me check if I've got this right. You appreciate being able to express your worries to me as that helps you to gain a new perspective. Did I get it right? Is there anything more?' Sender: 'Well, yes, I also mentioned that it helps me to calm down. Just having you listen to me when I share my worries, confirms to me that I am important to you. That makes me feel safe and loved.' Receiver: 'OK, let me check if I got it this time. You also feel safe and loved when I listen to your concerns. That confirms to you that you are important to me. Did I get it right? Is there anything else you want to add?' Sender: 'Yes, you've got it. And I think I expressed it all.' Receiver: 'Thank you. Let me summarise it all now. You felt saddened and frustrated this morning when I didn't appear to be listening to you sharing your concerns about work. That did upset you as our conversations help you to feel safe and loved. You also like hearing my perspective on the situation. Me being attentive when you talk makes you feel important and valuable to me. Did I get it all?' Sender: 'Yes, you got it.' This might seem a bit odd at first, but mirroring provides safety for a sender to express their experience of the situation and their deepest feelings about it. Mirroring provides evidence to the sender that the receiver is listening, and only in that state can we express ourselves in a non-offensive way (if I am being heard, there is no need to shout or shut down. It is safe to express how I feel). Moreover, mirroring and feeding back the information gives the receiver a chance to truly understand what is being said. It also creates clarity of the role – I don't need to fix anything or defend my position. At this point, my only job is to repeat as accurately as I can what is being said.

- *Validating* – in this step, the receiver is expected to validate that the things the sender is saying are making sense. The receiver does not necessarily need to agree with them, but their opinion on the matter should not be expressed at this point (they can do so later on when it is their turn to be a sender). I invite the receiver to truly try to see the world through the eyes of the sender here and allow multiple perceptions of the same situation. If you remember Chapter Three on personality, we all experience the world differently, and most issues arise from us being ignorant of the other person's perception of reality. We naturally tend to think that the world is as we perceive it, but each of us is *biased* in our perception, memory and recollection, based on our individual experiences. Therefore, it is physically impossible for two people to experience the situation in the same way. In validating the other person's experience, we honour and respect the way they experience the world (and why shouldn't we? Is the way I experience the world better than the way you do?). The receiver of the previous example could say, 'I get that when I was checking my phone this morning it must have appeared to you that I was not listening. And given that you expressed how important to you it is being able to talk things through with me, you would feel upset and frustrated in that setting. I get it. It makes sense.' If you notice, the receiver is not trying to defend their position – they are simply trying to see the situation as the sender might have, based on the things the sender shared. That just keeps the space for the sender to accept the feelings they have experienced and to feel that the receiver understands and accepts why they could have felt that way (validation).

- *Empathising* – once the validation step is completed, adding more emotional depth to it will create a feeling of connection. For that, the receiver needs to empathise with the *feelings* that the sender has shared – frustration, not being listened to, sadness. If the feelings have not been expressed very clearly, there is a chance to clarify that as well. Receiver: 'So given what you have expressed, I can imagine that you must have felt sad and frustrated because you didn't feel listened to this morning. Is that right?' Sender: 'Yes, I did. It really upset me. Thinking about it, it resembled the situation at work – I often feel invisible there, and that is the thing that frustrates me most.' Receiver: 'Oh I see, so you felt that me seeming disinterested in what you had to share almost confirmed the feeling you were experiencing at work? Am I right?' Sender: 'Exactly! I work really hard and have put a lot of training into my career, so it is very upsetting to feel as if I don't exist at work.' Receiver: 'Oh, I can imagine that it would be really upsetting to feel unvalued and invisible at work when you put so much time and effort into it. I can really get that. Is there anything else you want to share about it?' Then the sender has a choice to share anything else, or to complete the step: 'Thank you, I feel really heard by you. That means a lot to me.'

In a relationship, each partner should always have the opportunity to be the receiver and the sender. It requires both people to have the courage to be vulnerable and the willingness to reconnect. It can feel unnatural to start with, so it's best to start practising it with appreciation (such as sharing what you like most about your partner or letting them know that you really enjoyed the dinner they cooked last night) as triggering the amygdala makes it impossible for us not to react. Once the method has been practised enough to gain familiarity, a slightly more challenging conversation might be introduced (as discussed above). After that has been mastered, we accumulate increasingly more safety for the amygdala, allowing us to uncover our deepest feelings and deal with the situations that have caused us enormous amounts of suffering in the past. There is nothing more magical and healing than uncovering the parts of yourself that you feel uneasy about and the other person still being there for you and validating your experience. This might seem contradictory to the general wisdom – we often avoid validating and even shame so-called unwanted behaviours (either in others or in ourselves) in the hope that negative reinforcement will create a motivation to change. However, it achieves the opposite. If triggered, the amygdala creates reactive mammal-brain-dominant thinking and deactivates the PFC, which makes it impossible for us to truly hear another person, understand their point of view or feel empathy. That leads to all sorts of selfish reactive behaviours, which, if practised frequently, become our default reaction patterns in similar situations. Only by calming the amygdala and stimulating the PFC do we have a chance to change that. The tricky part is if only one person in the relationship wants to change the dynamics, or if people are too distant to require that level of intimacy in communication (such as business partners). In that situation, I would suggest looking at an alternative method which focuses on helping the person to meet their needs, called non-violent communication.

Principles of non-violent communication

American psychologist Marshall Rosenberg (2015) was puzzled by the amount of violence and conflict in the world. He made it his life's mission to find a way to help conflicting parties reach resolution. That resulted in a non-violent communication method, which provides us with tools for expressing our needs and wants effectively and clear guidelines for empathic listening. Even if only one partner learns these tools, they can gain a lot more insight into what the other person is truly trying to express and can respond in a non-violent manner. It is, of course, a lot easier if both people are willing to learn it, but in some cases that is not feasible.

Let's imagine Suzy and her teenage daughter Lilly are arguing endlessly and Suzy is willing to do anything to change that. Lilly, however, thinks that resolution will be naturally reached only if her mum can change her ways. Suzy feels criticised and stressed by Lilly's attitude and her resulting behaviours. Therefore, Suzy wants to learn to express her needs to Lilly in a peaceful way and is also willing to learn the root causes of Lilly's behaviour. Suzy needs to go through four steps to express herself effectively and learn to listen to Lilly in an empathic manner.

- *Observation* – in this stage it is important that Suzy identifies the objective facts free from evaluation or judgement (this part is hard to do, so might take a bit of practising). It could sound like this: 'Lilly, I have noticed that you have initiated conversations about our relationship over the last three days in the mornings before work.' It is important that Suzy just states the facts, rather than reading too much into these actions (such as 'You must not respect me and my work to start these conversations in the morning'). When we express judgement over these actions, we put another person into a defensive mode, which is doomed to result in withdrawal or attack from them.
- *Feelings* – in this step, Suzy wants to share how these situations make her *feel*. It is important to share the emotional component here, not thoughts about what that means.

So it could be something like: 'In these situations I feel stressed and frustrated.'

- *Needs* – we also need to identify what needs are not being met to cause these feelings. The list of needs can include the six needs we discussed before: safety/stability, variety, love/connection, significance, growth, contribution beyond yourself. We can expand the list, adding physical needs (food, rest); autonomy (freedom, independence); peace/harmony; and honesty. Once Suzy can identify which need or set of needs is being compromised to cause the feelings mentioned above, she can express it in as matter-of-fact, non-judgemental manner as possible: 'I have a need to connect with you and I want to be able to focus on that entirely when we discuss our relationship. I also have a need for safety, which I get from doing well at my job. I like to plan my work tasks in the morning so I can be as efficient as possible later on.' Suzy here is just explaining the things that are important to her without blaming Lilly for compromising it.

- *Request* – the last step is formulating a very clear and easy-to-follow request that will help Suzy to meet the needs expressed above: 'I would really like it if you set a specific time to connect and discuss our relationship when we don't have any competing matters. That would allow me to be in the best state to be fully present for you and your needs. Would you like to go out for dinner and discuss that after school today or would you prefer a different time or date? I would really like to spend some quality time together. Would you agree to that?' Here Suzy comes up with a very clear scenario, which has a low probability of triggering the amygdala – she states a few times how important Lilly and their connection is to her and that she does want to discuss the matter Lilly is initiating. She only suggests changing one thing – the timing of these conversations, providing a clear rationale for it. She also suggests an appealing way for them to connect – going out for a nice dinner, which will probably meet the need for significance and appreciation for Lilly.

As you can see, this requires Suzy to express herself in a much more amygdala-friendly way. Another thing Suzy can do is learn to listen to what needs Lilly is trying to meet with her behaviour – this is called listening with empathy and is somewhat similar to Imago listening. Let's imagine Lilly is resistant to change, and has a highly active amygdala, resulting in a mammal-brain-dominant attack. Here are five steps for how Suzy can listen to Lilly in an empathic and non-judgemental way:

- *Identify observations* – Lilly: 'You are always working and don't want to spend time with me.' Suzy: 'I am hearing that you notice me working long hours. How does that make you feel?' Here Suzy is helping Lilly to transition to the next stage rather than explaining that she needs to work hard to earn enough money for them, as that would change the focus of the conversation and take attention away from Lilly's feelings.
- *Identify feelings* – Lilly: 'You make me feel lonely and unimportant to you. I feel as if your work always takes first place before me.' Suzy: 'You are saying that you feel lonely and lack connection with me when I work long hours, is that what you mean?' As you can see, although Lilly is using blaming language, Suzy has a task to identify as accurately as possible the feelings that Lilly is talking about without taking it too personally. At the end of the day, the way people feel represents their internal world, not our intentions. So there is nothing to defend – just listen

and try to understand what the person is experiencing emotionally.

- *Empathise with the feeling* – feelings are universal. We can all relate to feelings even if we are not as in touch with some of them. So Suzy is now trying to remember the times when she felt lonely and lacked connection with her parents. This allows her to understand the state Lilly is in and connect with her at a deeper level. This step can be expressed or just related to in our minds. Suzy chooses to express it: 'Lilly, you must be suffering. I know how hard it is to feel lonely and lack connection to your parent.'

- *Identify the needs* – in this stage, Suzy is trying to identify from what has been already expressed what needs Lilly is lacking. In this case, it is connection and appreciation. Suzy double-checks though: 'Let me see if I've got it right. When I work long hours, you feel lonely and sad because you lack connection with me and want to feel important to me. Am I understanding it right?' Lilly is a bit puzzled as to why her mum is not reacting, but strangely feels calmed by feeling heard and understood by her. She nods.

- *Ask for a request* – the last step is for Suzy to figure out what actions would help Lilly feel connected and appreciated: 'How can I show you that I really care about you and want to be connected with you as well? What actions would make you feel that you are important to me?' Lilly: 'Well, you could stop bringing work home.' Suzy: 'Ah, OK, I can see that you would prefer seeing me having a better line between work and family life. To be honest, I would prefer that as well.' Lilly: 'Yeah, I think you would benefit from it too as you are always so tired and irritable in the evenings.' Suzy: 'That is true. When I bring work home, I do get very stressed and don't get enough time to relax. We probably should do something nice in the evenings together. What would you like to do?' Lilly: 'I don't know, maybe cooking together or watching a movie? And maybe on Wednesdays when I go to swimming you could stay there and go to the gym or a fitness class?' Suzy (laughing): 'I could do with adding some sports and healthier eating to my life actually. How about we start with cooking chilli con carne together today and I will see what classes they have at the gym during your swimming hours?' Lilly (smiling): 'Cool'.

I hope you can see in this example that there is a way to reduce the amount of times we get sucked into defending ourselves, which results in a lose-lose situation. Imagine if Suzy starts arguing with Lilly about her job and needing to work long hours to support them. How will that affect Lilly's need for connection? It will almost certainly deplete it even more, making her amygdala more alert and reactive. That will trigger Lilly to get more upset, which in turn will make Suzy feel guilty and more upset too. Suzy's needs for safety and connection with her daughter will sabotage that as well. And although our egos sometimes pull us into the desire to win an argument, we all lose at the end of it. So, this method provides us with a tool for creating safer conversations where we can get to the root cause of the behaviour and find a reasonable win-win solution. However, we first need to assess and tweak our internal dialogue in order to be able to be present, compassionate and PFC-dominant thinkers in conversations with others.

Internal communication

We all have a certain internal dialogue we use to assess the actions of others and ourselves. The thoughts we practise most frequently strengthen the brain networks that created them in the first place, creating a default pattern of inner dialogue. Of course, our state can influence it. For example, if we are hungry, dehydrated, fatigued or anxious we go through mammal-brain-dominant thinking patterns; while well rested and calm we have different dominant thoughts. When we talk about creating a non-violent and empowering dialogue, we need to assess what conversations happen in our minds too. Our mind chatter will ultimately change the way we feel, think and react around others, so it is a fundamentally important place to start. Let's look into our most dominant thoughts: what unmet needs do they indicate and how do we feel when we experience these needs not being met in a sufficient manner? Let's imagine Suzy's teenage daughter Lilly wants to learn to understand herself and reduce her anxiety and reactivity. Here is her uncensored inner chatter:

- 'I am useless and will never be able to have as successful a career as my mum.' This thought indicates that Lilly wants to get her significance from being successful in her career. She is still at school doing her A-levels and is ranked as one of the top students in the class but she lacks clarity on what to do next. Therefore, she envies her mum, who seems to know exactly what she wants career wise and is so good at it. By being 'useless' she means that she is lost and doesn't know how to fix it. She now needs to get a bit more specific on what exactly is missing and brainstorm some ideas to widen the horizons of her reactive mammal brain. 'I really don't know what career to choose, but I want to work with people, use my creativity and analytical skills together. However, most jobs are either creative or analytic, so I feel stuck. I need to really learn about the wider range of career options by the end of this term so I gain more clarity. Maybe Mum could help me to brainstorm a list of careers that would contain both components.' As you can see, thinking about the deeper issue, Lilly no longer feels resentful of her mum or competitive with her. She starts to get a desire to talk to her mum about it openly. At this point, it would be very important for her mum to be inquisitive and use non-directive coaching-like questions ('What would you dream job contain? What kind of people would you like to be surrounded by? Do you prefer a variety of tasks or routine?'). Suzy might even suggest doing the Demartini value questionnaire with Lilly, or at least tell her about it. That would help Lilly to gain more clarity about what is important to her and create a set of criteria for measuring each career option.

- 'My mum doesn't care about me' – perhaps we could use Byron Katie's The Work method to take a reality check of this statement. After watching a few workshops by Byron Katie on YouTube or reading her book, Lilly can do that herself or she can be guided through that process by a qualified coach.

1. *Is that true?* 'Yes, she doesn't want to spend time with me.'
2. She doesn't want to spend time with you and doesn't care about you. *Can you be absolutely sure that that is true?* 'No, I cannot be absolutely sure, but it seems that way.'
3. *How do you feel and what do you do when you believe that* 'My mum doesn't want to spend time with me and doesn't care about me'? 'I feel sad, lonely, unimportant. I start watching movies to escape these feelings; I can't really focus on my studies. Sometimes I even feel like sabotaging my grades to punish her for her lack of attention. Then I feel guilty for thinking that and start doing things to please her, like making her coffee or buying her a small gift. But none of it feels peaceful; it feels as if I need to win her love. It really consumes me.'
4. OK, our perceptions are biased on how we feel and what we fear. *Who would you be without the thought,* 'My mum

doesn't want to spend time with me and doesn't care about me'? 'Well, I would feel less sad when she is not around, I would be able to do other things and reach out to other people. I would be able to communicate to my mum when I want her to spend time with me as I wouldn't have a belief that she wouldn't want to do that. I would be able to focus on my schoolwork more and would probably be freer to make career choices that are well suited to me (rather than to please or punish her). I would feel lighter and happier. When we did spend time together, I would be a lot more fun as well.'

5. *Do you see a reason to drop this belief?* 'Yes, I can see that I can make much more out of my time with my mum when I don't have that belief. Also, I could focus on building connections with other people rather than expecting so much from my mum.'

6. *Turnarounds* (what are the alternative statements that could be as true or truer?):

   a. 'My mum does want to spend time with me and she does care about me' – can you find any evidence of that? 'Yes, I can actually. She is always interested in how my day went and will stay up all night with me if I need any help. She does also keep suggesting doing things together, so I think she does want to spend time together.'

   b. 'I don't want to spend time with my mum and don't care about her' – how does that sit with you? 'Oh wow, I can see that I am sometimes too busy with my after-school clubs and social gatherings to even notice if she wants to spend time with me (it's the same, I suppose, for her with her work, so probably it is not personal).'

    c. 'I don't want to spend time with me and don't care
      about me' – what do you think about that statement?
      'Yes, that's deep. I suppose all the insecurities are
      coming from within me. I sometimes seek to spend
      time with others to escape my negative mind chatter,
      almost like distracting myself. I suppose that does
      count as not wanting to spend time with the real me
      as I truly am with all these different thoughts. And I
      suppose I don't care as much about myself as about
      other people, so maybe I should learn to be more
      caring towards myself so I need less external input to
      calm me down.'

Challenging her inner dialogue, Lilly is getting into more objective reality and activating her PFC, which makes her less reactive and more resourceful.

Another way we can foster a more amygdala-friendly inner dialogue is by writing a gratitude or 'what went well today' list. In that, we point out to our amygdala what things are OK in our surroundings, giving us a chance to have a more balanced perception of the world. The amygdala will naturally still be able to notice things that are less than perfect, but at least there will be some positive things to balance that with. In a gratitude list, we can include very specific things that are meaningful to us. For example:

- Enjoyed a morning dog walk.
- Have received appreciation from a colleague for helping with their data analysis.
- Enjoyed lunch.
- Have had another day without a migraine.
- Have walked double the distance in comparison to yesterday.

This internal assessment of positive things allows us to feel more balanced and have a more objective view on where we stand. This is also important in communication with others – we often express things we are not happy with but fail to acknowledge and mention appreciation for one another.

Harmful interactions and better alternatives

To continue our discussions on Gottman's research (Gottman & Silver, 1994; Gottman et al., 2019), couples staying in the Apartment Lab for 24 hours were monitored having regular interactions and also doing assignments – discussing a pleasant, neutral and a topic they had disagreement about. During the entire time they were being filmed, their language was recorded, their heart rates were monitored and urine samples were taken to measure their levels of stress hormones. Other than that, it was like staying in a bed and breakfast. Data scientists analysed video and audio recordings and stress responses. They identified four types of interaction that were very harmful for relationships:

1. *Constant criticism* – being constantly dissatisfied with the actions or inactions of another person and feeling in the right to educate or 'fix' them (for example, 'You always spend money on meaningless shopping, what's wrong with you?'). A better alternative is *expressing this message in 'I' language* and pointing out the needs in you that are not being met by this behaviour: 'I am feeling worried about our financial situation. I have a need for safety and want to provide the same for our family. When I see our bank account depleting, it triggers fear in me. I know that we had some large expenses recently. Could we talk about it?'

2. *Unhelpful defence* – this involves reacting to criticism either with a counter attack: 'You buy things we don't need too,

and you are always late coming home from work' or self-victimisation: 'I just needed to buy a new watch. I would really like to have a supportive wife, who shares my dreams'. A better alternative is *taking responsibility* for your actions: 'Yes, I wanted to talk to you about it. I have seen this amazing watch, which is guaranteed to go up in value based on my research. I got an opportunity to buy one for a really good price and decided that there is no downside to it. Thinking about it now, I really should have discussed it with you before buying it. I will make sure to do it in the future so we are both on the same page. Thank you for pointing it out to me, that was inconsiderate and rushed from my side.'

3. *Disrespect and condemnation* – calling a person names that indicate that we look at that person as someone of lesser value or lower status. Gottman found this form of communication to be the best predictor of divorce as it indicates our core attitude towards that person. To continue on from the previous example, it would sound like this: 'You are such a selfish jerk, you always do what you want and are a completely irresponsible father and husband. I should never have married such a loser' (it does sound harsh, doesn't it?). There is no quick fix, but linking the values of that person to your own values as discussed in the previous chapter might help to elevate the status of that person in our minds. Healthy relationships require seeing the person at the same level and it is only our biased perception and desire for another person to be like us that blinds us to seeing their value and the benefit of them. What are the benefits to you, based on the things you truly value, of your partner spending a large amount of money on something that is important to them?

4. *Stone-walling* – this is lacking a response to the things the partner says or does. In relationships, we communicate

with words, body language and actions driven by a specific situation. When we stone-wall, we pretend the person is not there. That is surely guaranteed to trigger the amygdala response in the blanked person, as feeling connected is crucial for producing the feelings of safety essential for the mammal brain. As an alternative, we can communicate when we are not in a position to have a conversation: 'I am feeling really unwell at the moment as I am very stressed about my work and I do not have the space of mind to deal with anything else. Could we please have this conversation this evening when I can be fully present to hear what you want to share?'

Gottman also noticed that couples needed the minimal ratio of 5:1 between positivity and negativity to be OK. To have a very fulfilling and empowering relationship required the ratio to be more like 20:1. So this brings me to another important point – we need to learn to communicate our appreciation to each other even in simple day-to-day situations. We can use the Imago dialogue or non-violent communication methods to share appreciation in a way that feels meaningful to the other person. Let's end this chapter by discussing a few ideas on how we can introduce more positivity in communication:

- *Showing gratitude* – sharing gratitude of the things said or done (such as, 'I feel really grateful that we had a delicious and healthy dinner tonight. Thank you so much for cooking it') triggers the reward system to produce dopamine in both people, enhancing their happiness and wellbeing. Moreover, pointing positive things out will help to counteract the mind chatter of the amygdala, resulting in a more balanced perception of your relationships.
- *Showing appreciation* – similar to sharing gratitude, this can encompass the way the person is overall (e.g. 'I would like

to share how much I appreciate how affectionate you are in our relationship. I feel very loved by you when you hug me as soon as we see each other'). It is important to be honest and share appreciation for things that you truly value.

- *Being interested in their top three values* – once you have identified what three things are the most important to the person you are communicating with, you being supportive towards those values will feel very meaningful to them, even if it is asking about them and giving them the chance to share the thing they love with you (such as 'Have you learned anything new about watches today?').

- *Identifying their 'language of love'* – Gary Chapman, in his book *The 5 Love Languages* (2015), postulates that there are five languages of love (words, gifts, acts of service, quality time and physical touch) and each of us has a preference for which of them we are the most receptive to. It's just one way to point out the differences in preference we might have. Remember, your brain naturally tends to think that the other person is pretty much like you are. Therefore, it is important to learn about each other's preferences and then decide if that is the way you are willing to express your love and appreciation to that person. For example, my top two languages are physical touch and quality time, so I feel the most loved when we do things together. Matthew needs words or affirmation and really appreciates considerate gifts. Knowing this difference in preferences can help us to be the most effective in making another person feel special when we want to achieve that – I have spent lots of time (more than I would naturally be inclined to) choosing thoughtful gifts for Matthew for special occasions, and Matthew takes time off work so we can do things together on my birthday and other important days.

- *Asking questions* – this is the most effective way to show that another person is important to you. When anyone who is important to us finds the time get to know how we feel, what things we are interested in, and how things are going in various areas of our lives, we secrete oxytocin, the hormone of connection, trust and attachment. That makes us feel safe, reduces stress and increases brain plasticity, which helps us to deal with anything we are going through.

Last but not least, the most dominant way we express ourselves and listen to others becomes more pronounced with repeated use, making us more prone to do it again. Therefore, successful communication requires methodical repetition of expression and listening styles that do work well in order to override the ones we want to change.

Summary of Chapter Nine

Let's summarise the important points for effective communication:

1. Before a conversation, the PFC needs to be well replenished and the amygdala reasonably calm.
2. It's important to find amygdala-friendly ways of communicating, such as the Imago technique, where the person's experience is being listened to, mirrored, validated and empathised with.
3. We do engage in unhelpful communication patterns if we feel unheard, disrespected or deprived of having our other important needs met. Therefore, in communication it is important to figure out what specific needs we are trying to meet with our behaviour and communicate them in a direct and clear manner.

4. The way we think and express ourselves is largely influenced by our inner communication. Therefore, to be more kind and considerate to others we need to do the same for ourselves first.

5. Default communication patterns are caused by dominant brain networks, which get stronger over time with more practice. Only with consistent and regular practice of new ways of engaging will we create a lasting change in communication patterns.

CONCLUSION

I hope after reading this book you feel that change is possible. However, we can only create a voluntary lasting change if we work in accordance with what our brains need to create and strengthen new networks. These networks are required to create new behaviours, new emotional patterns and ensure healthier dynamics in our relationships. To create new networks, we need enough energy, replenishment, sleep, a healthy balance of brain chemistry, low levels of stress, and, most importantly, emotional safety. To strengthen these networks, we need to repeat new behaviours/patterns on a regular basis. Moreover, if we want to replace unwanted behaviours, we need to figure out what it is that we are getting from them and find better ways to meet these important needs. This naturally reduces our desire to engage in old behaviours, and subsequently weakens old networks from the reduced repetition. This activity is dependent on brain plasticity. Of course, change in each area is somewhat specific, so let's look at a brief overview of each chapter. To make the insights come to life, we will take my hypothetical client Emily through this process. First, let's assess how happy (on a scale of 1–10, with 1 being as bad as it gets and 10 being ecstatic) Emily is with each of the nine areas discussed in this book:

1. *Habits* – 6/10. Emily is happy with her physical health, exercises regularly and has stopped drinking alcohol

recently; she still struggles though with moderating her sugar intake, and eats lots of bread, which often makes her feel bloated.

2. *Emotions* – 4/10. Emily struggles with bouts of negativity and depressive moods; she beats herself up for feeling that way, as she knows her life is good.

3. *Personality* – 5/10. Although she feels as if she has come a long way, Emily still struggles with a pessimistic view of the world. Whenever she is called for a meeting with her boss, her first thought is that she will fire her.

4. *Productivity* – 5/10. Emily is dedicated to getting lots done in her job, but that unfortunately results in her working really long hours (even if she doesn't have to). At the end of work, she often struggles to switch off which affects her personal life, quality of sleep and emotional wellbeing.

5. *Brain health* – 4/10. Emily often feels low, and has brain fog and chronic anxiety. She often struggles to think as clearly as she used to.

6. *Decision-making* – 6/10. Currently Emily is pretty happy with her life. But when she needs to make an important decision, she tends to think about it endlessly until she is so wrapped up in her own thinking that she feels totally paralysed to make any decision in the end.

7. *Leadership* – 6/10. Emily's job requires long hours on the computer, interacting with customers and communicating strategies with her colleagues. She would like to be promoted to a more managerial role, but fears that she might not have what it takes for a leadership role.

8. *Relationships* – 5/10. She is in a committed relationship with her partner Daniel. They usually get on really well but have been experiencing some friction as both of them have been working from home. In disagreements, Daniel often switches off, which drives Emily crazy. In the heat

of the moment she often says things she later regrets and feels insane for doing so.

9. *Communication* – 6/10. Emily has a great group of friends and can express her thoughts and emotions well to them. She is also a great listener when friends need her help. Her communication in romantic relationship is similar as long as she and Daniel don't have disagreements. In arguments, Emily tends to experience huge bouts of anger and anxiety, creating impulsive accusations, counter-complaints and defensiveness.

As you can see, Emily scores around five in each of the areas, indicating that her life is bearable, but far from her sense of ideal. She has tried to change each of the areas by sheer willpower and determination, but often falls back into old habits. That yo-yo of deciding to change, putting lots of effort into creating change and then falling back into old habits (or failing to change, as Emily would call it) is having a really negative effect on her. She compares her life to those of others and feels even more desperate and depressed. Emily believes that she is fundamentally flawed. 'What is wrong with me?' she asks me, releasing a big sigh. So, let's take Emily through the ideas in this book chapter by chapter to gain insights on why she has found change so hard in the past and to see what her brain requires to make a lasting change.

1. *Changing habits.* After an assessment of her day-to-day life it is clear that Emily is overstretched. She takes real pride in always being busy, making it hard for her to prioritise taking breaks. After establishing that her PFC is required to create change and that the functioning of this area gets compromised when we are overly tired, she comes up with the plan of starting a new habit in the morning, when her PFC is still fresh. We decide to begin with one change at

a time and Emily chooses eating healthier, so introduces making eggs for breakfast as an alternative to skipping breakfast or grabbing a pastry and coffee at the train station. To increase her motivation, I ask Emily to write a list of 50 benefits of her starting this habit and 50 drawbacks of not doing that. With a bit of probing she ends up with two big lists and a new perspective on this change. Her initial thought of stopping eating pastries was associated with pain. However, her new habit triggers associations of pleasure (like looking great in her skinny jeans, having a sharper focus in her morning meetings, saving the money she was spending on pastry and coffee in the station for a holiday), while the old habit is now associated with pain (such as head fog and a bloated stomach). She realises that she often uses sugar as emotional escapism when she is anxious, so we come up with an alternative – writing in a journal about her feelings instead. Emily likes writing and wants to gain more insights into her anxiety, so that is appealing to her and she buys a beautiful new notebook specifically dedicated to it. To avoid triggering her amygdala due to big changes all at once, Emily is changing only her breakfast habit – she will address lunch and dinner habits at a later date. That makes the task a lot more manageable. To create well-established networks, Emily commits to a new healthy breakfast habit every morning with the exception of Sunday when she likes to go out for pancakes in the local café with her niece. This plan feels manageable and rather exciting to Emily.

2. *Changing emotions.* After Emily has tackled changing her food habits, we start working on her emotional patterns. The first step is to gradually gain awareness of what each emotion is telling her. We go through all of the eight emotions and identify when Emily is experiencing them. Emily

has spent so long trying to suppress unwanted emotions and labelling them as bad that it takes a while for her to accept that they are just a normal part of her mammal brain functioning. She starts observing the situations that precede these emotions and becomes skilful at identifying what her mammal brain is trying to tell her. She finds that anger, anxiety and sadness are often caused by situations lacking safety and stability and is trying to provide that to a greater extent for her mammal brain by developing helpful habits. She also gets great relief learning about amygdala-dominant and PFC-dominant thinking – 'So I am not crazy after all!' she shares after I explain that it is all part of normal brain functioning. Then we design a plan of how not to get carried away with making important decisions when her amygdala is being triggered and starts to hijack her PFC. Emily commits to taking a 15-minute break in these situations. She gradually starts implementing this in her relationship too. After a while, Emily starts examining the inner thoughts that trigger her amygdala too by using The Work method, which, after a bit of practice, becomes a straightforward tool to challenge unhelpful and outdated beliefs. Emily chooses each Sunday afternoon as her time to re-assess her emotional patterns and to do The Work or other PFC-dominant techniques to challenge her thinking. Gradually, her negative feelings are replaced with feelings of inner peace and even joy, but it does require regular intentional work. Emily starts with writing in a journal about her emotions, investigating the triggers and gradually accepting that all emotions are needed and provide valuable feedback. She follows this with building safety-inducing habits, practising time-off when her amygdala has been triggered, and challenging her inner beliefs.

3. *Changing personality.* After we address her emotional patterns and start working to change them, a lot of her complaints about her personality traits recede. Learning about biased perception helps Emily to gain a more open-minded view on challenging her perceptions. We go through the Demartini method in assessing what things Emily truly values. That helps her to gain insights into which goals are truly meaningful to her and which ones she has accumulated due to subordination to other people's values. The combination of understanding her highest values and seeing how she has been trying to make changes that weren't really important to her (such as building hew own business as her sister did or constantly learning new things as her father encouraged her to do) takes some weight off her shoulders and helps Emily to get a much clearer idea of what specific goals are well aligned with what she wants to achieve in her life. Looking at the definitions of the fixed and growth mindsets, Emily starts to laugh. 'I often fall into fixed mindset and focus on the things that are not in my control, but for my friends and family I offer great growth mindset-dominant support.' We agree that she can do that for herself and she writes a list of things that are in her control to focus on.

4. *Changing productivity.* Emily initially believed that working non-stop and multitasking was helping her to get more things done. After we challenge that belief with neuroscience insights, Emily admits that she does get very stressed when she tries to juggle lots of tasks and her brain starts to become fatigued, making it harder to stay efficient and sharp in the afternoons. Although still trying to focus solely on work, Emily takes much longer to craft sound emails and to handle customer requests after 2 p.m. When she does the calculations, she is astonished to see that her

efficiency is reduced by at least half if not three times in the second part of her day. Emily decides to try the Pomodoro Technique to train her attention span and subsequently manages to reduce multitasking. Although she still has a resistance to taking breaks, Emily comes up with a good idea – moving meetings, which she finds very easy to focus on, to the afternoons rather than the mornings. Carrying out a procrastination assessment, Emily is surprised to find that a lot of her overworking comes from an inability to say no and perfectionism, which often leaves her feeling exhausted yet unable to switch off. It leads to her being too fatigued to focus on the task, making her more prone to distractions such as checking her phone and emails, reading the news and picking up easy but low-priority tasks. Emily writes all the tasks down and sorts them into four quadrants based on their urgency and importance. Then we cross out all low-priority tasks that could be delegated and address how to say no to them in the future. We also develop a strategy on how to gain significance and connection (the needs Emily was meeting by saying yes and in her perfectionism) in other ways.

5. *Changing brain health.* Emily does lots of exercise and eats a fairly healthy diet. However, she identifies that she is driving her brain into an overly excitatory state by consuming large amounts of stimulants like sugar and coffee. Moreover, she agrees that it is about time that she develops better working habits and starts taking decent breaks to give her PFC a chance to recover and replenish. She realises that most of her coffee and chocolate consumption happens after lunch, so we come up with an idea – instead of having lunch at her desk, she agrees to go for a light jog or at least a brisk walk for 30 minutes during her lunch break. After gentle exercise, she naturally feels relaxed and her brain is well

replenished with oxygen-rich blood. Also, after putting effort and time into exercise she naturally makes better food choices, so she will grab soup or a salad from a healthy café next door. Emily will try to avoid dairy and gluten at lunchtime to see if it makes a difference in reducing brain fog. We agree to keep the coffee for now, but limit this to only one cup at lunchtime. Sleep is another area that requires improvement. Eliminating coffee intake after 1 p.m. is likely to make a difference. Also, Emily often checks her emails after dinner and sometimes gets carried away working until bedtime. It is not surprising that it causes her mind to race, she has an inability to switch off, and it takes her ages to drift off to sleep. After all the other changes are successfully implemented and become new habits, we tackle this – we work on her motives of wanting to check emails so late and challenge any beliefs around that using Byron Katie's The Work method (Katie & Mitchell, 2002). Then we design an alternative evening routine, replacing working-on-the-laptop time with anything that feels pleas-ant for Emily (it is easier to replace the habit if the new habit triggers reward centres as well or is better than the old one!) – watching a movie (not ideal, but better than replying to client inquiries), dinner with a friend, a walk by the river, chatting to her mum on FaceTime, doing crafts, reading a book.

6. *Changing decision-making.* After learning about the fast and experience-based decision-making System I and rational but slow decision-making System II, Emily goes through the list of important decisions she has made in recent years and labels which system was the most helpful for her in making that decision. A lot of personal choices, such as choosing which people to spend time with and which hobbies to pursue, were successfully made by a mammal-brain-driven

gut feeling; while others, such as which country to live in, required methodological step-by-step assessment. However, most of the challenging decisions, such as who to date so as to avoid past mistakes, but still have a spark, required a combination of both systems. Emily acknowledges that she often doesn't trust her emotions when she is making professional choices, with the result that she often gets stuck in analysis paralysis. That changes, however, after she starts keeping a journal of her emotions and what things have triggered them – they suddenly seem a lot more valid and important than she has ever allowed herself to accept. Emily agrees to observe her emotions at work and see if there is any clear pattern emerging that could help her make quicker decisions.

7. *Changing leadership.* Learning about dissonant and resonant modes, Emily recognises that she is often dissonant while focusing on work-related tasks in order to get them done efficiently. That does sometimes get in the way of her gaining an understanding of her colleagues' points of view during meetings as she struggles to switch from a dissonant to a resonant mode. She is usually proficient in the resonant style with her friends and during informal time with colleagues. Emily realises that if she wants to gain a leadership post in her workplace, she must start practising resonant style in the group meetings, to allow her to get to know her colleagues' way of thinking and to aid better collaboration. She also expresses her aspirations to her line manager and asks if she can start supervising somebody officially to build up that skillset. To her surprise, her line manager is very pleased with that as she is overstretched with her supervising responsibilities and assigns Emily a supervisee. With practice, Emily finds the right balance of dissonant and resonant styles of supervision, providing her

supervisee with both a good environment to get analytical tasks done effectively and a creative and inspiring place to share ideas and collaborate with others during the meetings.

8. *Changing relationships.* Overall, Emily is very happy with her relationship and feels that Daniel is the guy she wants to spend the rest of her life with. After comparing her relationship dynamics to her family of origin, Emily realises that she is sometimes overly independent (avoidant attachment style) and does not allow Daniel to truly be there for her. We start working on inner child healing to educate her amygdala that the world is a much safer place than she learned about as a child. We work on each outdated belief that her mammal brain is still holding on to and challenge them with the PFC one after another, replacing them with more accurate alternatives (again, using Byron Katie's The Work method (Katie & Mitchell, 2002)). That allows Emily to open up more to Daniel about sensitive topics, creating more emotional intimacy between them. Seeing that Daniel not only doesn't run away, but also opens up more in that amygdala-safe space, Emily gets to know Daniel at a much deeper level too, strengthening their connection and trust even more. They also learn more about each other's top three values and link them, which helps them see each other as the best possible partner for each other, creating more appreciation and reducing previous conflict.

9. *Changing communication.* Emily realises that she is quick to be offended. She learns that her need for respect is extremely important to her in her relationship and learns to express it in a non-violent communication way. Moreover, she is learning to listen to the needs Daniel is expressing when he communicates with her. They are both open-minded in trying the Imago method, although it does still feel a bit unnatural at this stage. They are practising one Imago

dialogue a week and are getting more and more skilled at it. They are trying to express more positivity in their interactions by discussing what things they have enjoyed each day, and are asking open-ended questions to learn about each other's experience of that day. Interestingly, that reminds them that although they have a lot in common, they are still two different people, so assumptions of how the other person thinks or what the other person meant should be avoided and the direct questions lead to a true understanding of each other. Both Daniel and Emily feel more visible in their relationship and more accepted for who they truly are. They still do have disagreements, but after they have introduced a 15-minute break each time things start to escalate, Emily no longer exhibits huge anger outbursts and Daniel does not need to switch off as much. They are getting better at respecting each other's emotional and mental states, creating better boundaries and healthier arguments when they do happen.

Each of us has such a special and unique brain, so I hope you will tailor the content of this book to best aid your individual situation. Each brain is incredible and capable of amazing things and I hope this book has helped you to get to know yours better. I hope you'll have a new deep respect and acceptance for your brain so you can achieve change according to how your brain truly is rather than working against it. Most issues in our lives happen when we don't accept the reality and make plans based on how we wish ourselves to be rather than who we truly are. That's a sure way of getting lost. I hope you'll now discover more of who you (and your brain) are and strip away the layers that don't belong to you. You are perfect, just the way you are. Ironically, when you accept that, you can create meaningful change to develop habits that serve you better, experience more pleasant emotional patterns, make decisions that lead to more fulfilment, and develop relationships that are special and worthy of all the work we need to put in to create healthy and empowering communication patterns. I am with you each step of the journey, so feel free to read this book more than once, as different insights will resonate with you at different times. I hope that learning about your magnificent and crazy brain helps you love yourself a tad more too. You are awesome!

A LETTER FROM GABIJA

First of all, thank you for choosing to read my book *Why the F*ck Can't I Change?* I hope you have learned some interesting brain facts and valuable techniques to aid you in your journey of self-discovery. If you did enjoy this book and want to keep updated with my latest activities, just sign up at the following link (your email address will not be shared with third parties and you can unsubscribe at any time):

http://thread-books.com/sign-up

This book is a merging of my explorations doing neuroscience research, coaching business and individual clients, and delivering applied neuroscience workshops for companies and the general public. On this journey I have learned that a good balance between brain facts, relatable examples and practical, relevant tools is not an easy one to find and it required lots of tweaking along the way. I hope you find that the content of this book helps you to get to know your brain, understand the reasons why you get stuck and provides you with practical tools for moving forward.

I would really appreciate it if you could write me a review, as this helps readers to discover this book for the first time. Also, I'd love to hear your insights from reading this book and answer any questions you may still have. So feel free to contact me on Facebook, Twitter, LinkedIn or my website.

Wishing you a well-functioning PFC and a calm amygdala!
Gabija

empoweryourbrain

@supergcoaching

phd-gabija-toleikyte

www.mybrainduringtheday.com

ABBREVIATIONS

- ANS – autonomic nervous system
- BBB – blood-brain barrier
- BDNF – brain-derived neurotropic factor
- CBT – cognitive behavioural therapy
- DMN – default mode network
- GABA – gamma amino butyric acid
- IA – inner adult
- IC – inner child
- IP – inner parent
- LGN – lateral geniculate nucleus
- LTP – long-term potentiation
- MNS – mirror neuron system
- NAcc – Nucleus accumbens
- non-REM – non-rapid eye-movement stage of sleep
- PFC – prefrontal cortex
- PSNS – parasympathetic nervous system
- REM –rapid eye-movement stage of sleep
- SNS – sympathetic nervous system
- SRIs – serotonin reuptake inhibitors
- TA – transactional analysis
- TPN – task-positive network
- VTA – ventral tegmental area

REFERENCES
AND FURTHER READING

Chapter One

1. Book describing habit loops in great depth
   Duhigg, C. (2013). *The Power of Habit: Why We Do What We Do, and How to Change*. Random House Books.
2. Brilliant book summarising multiple research studies on brain plasticity in action
   Doidge, N. (2008). *The Brain that Changes Itself: Stories of Personal Triumph from the Frontiers of Brain Science*. Penguin Books.
3. Original work of the Triune Brain model
   MacLean, P. D. (1990). *The Triune Brain in Evolution: Role in Paleocerebral Functions*. Plenum Press.
4. Research paper discussing the ways we can measure metabolism in different areas of the brain
   Barros, L. F., Bolaños, J. P., Bonvento, G., Bouzier-Sore, A. K., Brown, A., Hirrlinger, J., Kasparov, S., Kirchhoff, F., Murphy, A. N., Pellerin, L., Robinson, M. B., & Weber, B. (2018). Current technical approaches to brain energy metabolism. *Glia, 66*(6), 1138–1159. https://doi.org/10.1002/glia.23248
5. Marshmallow test in children

Mischel, W., Shoda, Y., & Rodriguez, M. I. (1989). Delay of gratification in children. *Science, 244*(4907), 933–938. https://doi.org/10.1126/science.2658056

6. Review article on activity-dependent brain plasticity
Butz, M., Wörgötter, F., & van Ooyen, A. (2009). Activity-dependent structural plasticity. *Brain research reviews, 60*(2), 287–305. https://doi.org/10.1016/j.brainresrev.2008.12.023

7. The role of the reward centers of the brain in the motivation of behaviours
Schultz, W. (2015). Neuronal reward and decision signals: From theories to data. *Physiological Reviews, 95*(3), 853–951. https://doi.org/10.1152/physrev.00023.2014

8. Review of short-term and long-term brain plasticity
Di Filippo, M., Picconi, B., Tantucci, M., Ghiglieri, V., Bagetta, V., Sgobio, C., Tozzi, A., Parnetti, L., & Calabresi, P. (2009). Short-term and long-term plasticity at corticostriatal synapses: Implications for learning and memory. *Behavioural Brain Research, 199*(1), 108–118. https://doi.org/10.1016/j.bbr.2008.09.025

9. Review article on adult neurogenesis
Cameron, H. A., & Glover, L. R. (2015). Adult neurogenesis: Beyond learning and memory. *Annual Review of Psychology, 66*, 53–81. https://doi.org/10.1146/annurev-psych-010814-015006

Chapter Two

1. Book by world-leading amygdala researcher on anxiety and fear and how they change our thinking (amygdala hijack of the PFC)
LeDoux, J. E. (2016). *Anxious: Using the Brain to Understand and Treat Fear and Anxiety*. Penguin Books.

2. Great book describing the origins of our emotions
   Panksepp, J., & Biven, L. (2012). *The Archaeology of Mind: Neuroevolutionary Origins of Human Emotions*. W. W. Norton & Co.

3. Book on the power of positive affirmations to soothe your amygdala (can also be used for inner child healing) – some people love it while others find it too soft, but worth checking out
   Hay, L. L. (1984). *You Can Heal Your Life*. Hay House.

4. A very practical book taking you through The Work method to challenge your thoughts and inner beliefs
   Katie, B., & Mitchell, S. (2002). *Loving What Is: Four Questions That Can Change Your Life*. Rider.

5. Book on how values hierarchy influences your motivation
   Demartini, J. F. (2013). *The Values Factor: The Secret to Creating an Inspired and Fulfilling Life*. Berkley Books.

6. Review article on different types of emotions, how we experience them and the brain areas associated with them
   Barrett, L. F., Mesquita, B., Ochsner, K. N., & Gross, J. J. (2007). The experience of emotion. *Annual Review of Psychology, 58*, 373–403. https://doi.org/10.1146/annurev.psych.58.110405.085709

7. An article showing bodily maps of emotions
   Volynets, S., Glerean, E., Hietanen, J. K., Hari, R., & Nummenmaa, L. (2020). Bodily maps of emotions are culturally universal. *Emotion, 20*(7), 1127–1136. https://doi.org/10.1037/emo0000624

8. A comprehensive review of insula research
   Nieuwenhuys, R. (2012). The insular cortex: A review. *Progress in brain research, 195*, 123–163. https://doi.org/10.1016/B978-0-444-53860-4.00007-6

9. Review of the involvement of the sympathetic and para-sympathetic nervous systems in emotions
Kreibig, S. D. (2010). Autonomic nervous system activity in emotion: A review. *Biological psychology, 84*(3), 394–421. https://doi.org/10.1016/j.biopsycho.2010.03.010

10. ABC(DE) model in cognitive behavioural therapy
Ellis, A. (1991). The revised ABC's of rational-emotive therapy (RET). *Journal of Rational-Emotive and Cognitive-Behavior Therapy, 9*, 139–172. https://doi.org/10.1007/BF01061227

11. Research article on using gratitude and mindfulness interventions
O'Leary, K., & Dockray, S. (2015). The effects of two novel gratitude and mindfulness interventions on well-being. *Journal of Alternative and Complementary Medicine, 21*(4), 243–245. https://doi.org/10.1089/acm.2014.0119

Chapter Three

1. Book on how to determine your values hierarchy and how it influences various areas of your life
Demartini, J. F. (2013). *The Values Factor: The Secret to Creating an Inspired and Fulfilling Life*. Berkley Books.

2. Book describing research on fixed and growth mindsets
Dweck, C. S. (2017). *Mindset – Updated Edition: Changing the Way Your Think to Fulfil Your Potential*. Robinson.

3. Genetic and environmental factors in personality development
Briley, D. A., & Tucker-Drob, E. M. (2014). Genetic and environmental continuity in personality development: A meta-analysis. *Psychological Bulletin, 140*(5), 1303–1331. https://doi.org/10.1037/a0037091

4. An in-depth article on the hereditability factors of personality
Sanchez-Roige, S., Gray, J. C., MacKillop, J., Chen, C. H., & Palmer, A. A. (2018). The genetics of human personality. *Genes, Brain, and Behavior, 17*(3), e12439. https://doi.org/10.1111/gbb.12439

5. A review on the new emerging field of epigenetics and environmental factors that affect which genes are being used
Pinel, C., Prainsack, B., & McKevitt, C. (2018). Markers as mediators: A review and synthesis of epigenetics literature. *BioSocieties, 13,* 276–303. https://doi.org/10.1057/s41292-017-0068-x

6. A brilliant overview on the brain areas involved in different aspects of perception and learning
The Society for Neuroscience. (2018). *Brain Facts: A Primer on the Brain and Nervous System.* The Society for Neuroscience.
Free download available here: www.brainfacts.org/the-brain-facts-book

7. A review on bottom-up and top-down modulation of how we perceive the world
Choi, I., Lee, J. Y., & Lee, S. H. (2018). Bottom-up and top-down modulation of multisensory integration. *Current opinion in neurobiology, 52,* 115–122. https://doi.org/10.1016/j.conb.2018.05.002

8. A research study on growth and fixed mindsets in children
Haimovitz, K., & Dweck, C. S. (2017). The origins of children's growth and fixed mindsets: New research and a new proposal. *Child development, 88*(6), 1849–1859. https://doi.org/10.1111/cdev.12955

9. A great article summarising research on mindsets and their applications in practice

Dweck, C. S., & Yeager, D. S. (2019). Mindsets: A view from two eras. *Perspectives on Psychological Science, 14*(3), 481–496. https://doi.org/10.1177/1745691618804166

10. A review article on metaplasticity (changes in brain plasticity depending on what we do)
Müller-Dahlhaus, F., & Ziemann, U. (2015). Metaplasticity in human cortex. *The Neuroscientist, 21*(2), 185–202. https://doi.org/10.1177/1073858414526645

Chapter Four

1. A great book on the habits of highly effective people (such as putting tasks into four quadrants based on urgency and importance)
Covey, S. R. (2020). *The 7 Habits of Highly Effective People: 30th Anniversary Edition*. Simon & Schuster.

2. Book by the creator of the Pomodoro Technique
Cirillo, F. (2016). *The Pomodoro Technique: The Life-Changing Time Management System*. Virgin Digital.

3. A book on six types of procrastinators
Sapadin, L. (2011). *How to Beat Procrastination in the Digital Age*. Psychwisdom Publishing.

4. Dorsal and ventral attention systems in the brain
Vossel, S., Geng, J. J., & Fink, G. R. (2014). Dorsal and ventral attention systems: Distinct neural circuits but collaborative roles. *The Neuroscientist, 20*(2), 150–159. https://doi.org/10.1177/1073858413494269

5. Limitations of multitasking
Skaugset, M. L., Farrell, S., Carney, M., Wolff, M., Santen, S. A., Perry, M., & Cico, S. J. (2016). Can you multitask? Evidence and limitations of task switching and multitasking in emergency medicine. *Annals of Emergency*

Medicine, 68(2), 189–195. https://doi.org/10.1016/j.annemergmed.2015.10.003

6. Article summarising different types of memory and the brain structures responsible for them
Budson, A. E., & Price, B. H. (2005). Memory dysfunction. *The New England Journal of Medicine, 352*(7), 692–699. https://doi.org/10.1056/NEJMra041071

7. Effects of exercise on brain plasticity
Marais, L., Stein, D. J., & Daniels, W. M. (2009). Exercise increases BDNF levels in the striatum and decreases depressive-like behavior in chronically stressed rats. *Metabolic brain disease, 24*(4), 587–597. https://doi.org/10.1007/s11011-009-9157-2

8. Study showing adult neurogenesis in the dentate gyrus brain structure
Abbott, L. C., & Nigussie, F. (2020). Adult neurogenesis in the mammalian dentate gyrus. *Anatomia, Histologia, Embryologia, 49*(1), 3–16. https://doi.org/10.1111/ahe.12496

9. Review article on changing memories (memory reconsolidation)
Haubrich, J., & Nader, K. (2018). Memory reconsolidation. *Current Topics in Behavioral Neurosciences, 37*, 151–176. https://doi.org/10.1007/7854_2016_463

10. Study about incorporating false memories
Hyman, I. E., Jr., & Billings, F. J. (1998). Individual differences and the creation of false childhood memories. *Memory, 6*(1), 1–20. https://doi.org/10.1080/741941598

Chapter Five

1. An amazing book on human behaviour
Sapolsky, R. M. (2018). *Behave: The Biology of Humans at Our Best and Worst*. Vintage.

2. Brilliant book on sleep research
Walker, M. P. (2018). *Why We Sleep: The New Science of Sleep and Dreams*. Penguin.

3. Book on brain inflammation as a potential factor in some cases of depression
Bullmore, E. (2019). *The Inflamed Mind: A Radical New Approach to Depression*. Short Books.

4. Review article describing different neurotransmitters
Hyman, S. E. (2005). Neurotransmitters. *Current biology, 15*(5), PR154–R158. https://doi.org/10.1016/j.cub.2005.02.037

5. Effects of environmental enrichment on brain plasticity
van Praag, H., Kempermann, G., & Gage, F. H. (2000). Neural consequences of environmental enrichment. *Nature Reviews Neuroscience, 1*(3), 191–198. https://doi.org/10.1038/35044558

6. Dendritic branch of the PFC and amygdala neurons morphology in stress
McEwen, B. S., Nasca, C., & Gray, J. D. (2016). Stress effects on neuronal structure: Hippocampus, amygdala, and prefrontal cortex. *Neuropsychopharmacology, 41*(1), 3–23. https://doi.org/10.1038/npp.2015.171

7. Original findings on childhood schizophrenia in celiac disease patients
Bender L. (1953). Childhood schizophrenia. *The Psychiatric Quarterly, 27*(4), 663–681. https://doi.org/10.1007/BF01562517

8. Research on the neurological effects of celiac disease and gluten sensitivity
Jackson, J. R., Eaton, W. W., Cascella, N. G., Fasano, A., & Kelly, D. L. (2012). Neurologic and psychiatric manifestations of celiac disease and gluten sensitivity. *Psychiatric Quarterly, 83*(1), 91–102. https://doi.org/10.1007/s11126-011-9186-y

9. Research article on 'leaky gut'
   Mu, Q., Kirby, J., Reilly, C. M., & Luo, X. M. (2017).
   Leaky gut as a danger signal for autoimmune diseases.
   Frontiers in Immunology, 8, 598. https://doi.org/10.3389/
   fimmu.2017.00598

10. Review article on experiments of the reward system
    Kringelbach, M. L., & Berridge, K. C. (2010). The func-
    tional neuroanatomy of pleasure and happiness. *Discovery
    Medicine, 9*(49), 579–587.

11. Review article on glutamate (includes glutamate excitotoxicity)
    Platt S. R. (2007). The role of glutamate in central nervous
    system health and disease – A review. *The Veterinary
    Journal, 173*(2), 278–286. https://doi.org/10.1016/j.
    tvjl.2005.11.007

Chapter Six

1. Original book describing the dual processing theory of fast
   and slow thinking
   Kahneman, D. (2011). *Thinking, Fast and Slow*. Penguin.

2. Neuroscience research-based book on how emotions are
   incorporated in even rational decision-making
   Damasio, A. R. (2006). *Descartes' Error: Emotion, Reason
   and the Human Brain*. Vintage.

3. Great book covering original research on the irrationality
   of our decisions
   Ariely, D. (2009). *Predictably Irrational: The Hidden Forces
   that Shape Our Decisions*. Harper.

4. Book on expertise-based fast decisions
   Gladwell, M. (2006). *Blink: The Power of Thinking Without
   Thinking*. Penguin.

5. Great book on how to embrace serendipity in your decisions
   Busch, C. (2020). *The Serendipity Mindset: The Art and Science of Creating Good Luck*. Penguin Life.

6. A book summarising great research on the optimism bias
   Sharot, T. (2012). *The Optimism Bias: Why We're Wired to Look on the Bright Side*. Robinson.

7. Book describing different types of biases
   Gilovich, T., Griffin, D., & Kahneman, D. (2002). *Heuristics and Biases: The Psychology of Intuitive Judgement*. Cambridge University Press.

8. Original work by Tversky and Kahneman on biases
   Tversky, A., & Kahneman, D. (1974). Judgment under uncertainty: Heuristics and biases. *Science, 185*(4157), 1124–1131. https://doi.org/10.1126/science.185.4157.1124

9. Anchoring experiment with social security number and bidding price
   Chapman, G. B., & Johnson, E. J. (1999). Anchoring, activation, and the construction of values. *Organizational Behavior and Human Decision Processes, 79*(2), 115–153. https://doi.org/10.1006/obhd.1999.2841

10. An experiment on the temperature of coffee cups influencing judgements on personality
    Williams, L. E., & Bargh, J. A. (2008). Experiencing physical warmth promotes interpersonal warmth. *Science, 322*(5901), 606–607. https://doi.org/10.1126/science.1162548

11. An experiment on words associated with elderly in scrambled word tasks affecting walking speed
    Bargh, J. A., Chen, M., & Burrows, L. (1996). Automaticity of social behavior: Direct effects of trait construct and stereotype activation on action. *Journal of Personality and Social Psychology, 71*(2), 230–244. https://doi.org/10.1037//0022-3514.71.2.230

12. Damasio's study with vmPFC patients and the Iowa gambling task
Bechara, A., Damasio, H., Tranel, D., & Damasio, A. R. (1997). Deciding advantageously before knowing the advantageous strategy. *Science, 275*(5304), 1293–1295. https://doi.org/10.1126/science.275.5304.1293

Chapter Seven

1. Book on resonant and dissonant leadership styles
Boyatzis, R., & McKee, A. (2005). *Resonant Leadership: Renewing Yourself and Connecting with Others Through Mindfulness, Hope and Compassion.* Harvard Business Review Press.

2. Book describing the effects of oxytocin for trust
Zak, P. J. (2013). *The Moral Molecule: How Trust Works.* Plume Books.

3. Book describing why the resonant mode is necessary to help people change
Boyatzis, R., Smith, M. L., & Van Oosten, E. (2019). *Helping People Change: Coaching with Compassion for Life-long Learning and Growth.* Harvard Business Review Press.

4. Great book on the GROW model of coaching
Whitmore, J. (2009). *Coaching for Performance: GROWing People, Performance and Purpose.* Nicholas Brealey Publishing.

5. Review article on DMN
Mak, L. E., Minuzzi, L., MacQueen, G., Hall, G., Kennedy, S. H., & Milev, R. (2017). The default mode network in healthy individuals: A systematic review and meta-analysis. *Brain Connectivity, 7*(1), 25–33. https://doi.org/10.1089/brain.2016.0438

6. Research on TPN and DMN in dissonant and resonant leadership
Boyatzis, R. E., Rochford, K., & Jack, A. I. (2014). Antagonistic neural networks underlying differentiated leadership roles. *Frontiers in Human Neuroscience, 8*, 114. https://doi.org/10.3389/fnhum.2014.00114

7. Another study by Jack and Boyatzis looking at how dissonant and resonant styles in coaching/mentoring affected people's behaviour and brain activity
Jack, A. I., Boyatzis, R. E., Khawaja, M. S., Passarelli, A. M., & Leckie, R. L. (2013). Visioning in the brain: An fMRI study of inspirational coaching and mentoring. *Social Neuroscience, 8*(4), 369–384. https://doi.org/10.1080/17470919.2013.808259

8. Review article on the mirror neuron system
Rizzolatti, G., & Craighero, L. (2004). The mirror-neuron system. *Annual Review of Neuroscience, 27*, 169–192. https://doi.org/10.1146/annurev.neuro.27.070203.144230

9. Effects of oxytocin on social functioning
Jones, C., Barrera, I., Brothers, S., Ring, R., & Wahlestedt, C. (2017). Oxytocin and social functioning. *Dialogues in Clinical Neuroscience, 19*(2), 193–201. https://doi.org/10.31887/DCNS.2017.19.2/cjones

10. The stress response in the body and the brain
McEwen B. S. (2007). Physiology and neurobiology of stress and adaptation: Central role of the brain. *Physiological Reviews, 87*(3), 873–904. https://doi.org/10.1152/physrev.00041.2006

11. Article on how oxytocin helps to counteract the stress response
Winter, J., & Jurek, B. (2019). The interplay between oxytocin and the CRF system: Regulation of the stress response. *Cell and Tissue Research, 375*(1), 85–91. https://doi.org/10.1007/s00441-018-2866-2

Chapter Eight

1. Great book describing why we are attracted to certain people (Imago theory)
   Hendrix, H. (2020). *Getting the Love You Want Revised Edition: A Guide for Couples*. Simon & Schuster.

2. Book covering John Gottman's research on relationship dynamics and the outcome of marriage
   Gottman, J. (2018). *The Seven Principles for Making Marriage Work: A Practical Guide from the International Bestselling Relationship Expert*. Orion Spring.

3. Accessible book on transactional analysis
   Lapworth, P., and Sills, C. (2011). *An Introduction to Transactional Analysis: Helping People Change*. SAGE Publications.

4. In-depth book on transactional analysis
   Berne, E. (2015). *Transactional Analysis in Psychotherapy: A Systematic Individual and Social Psychiatry*. Martino Fine Books.

5. Great book on how childhood experiences influence brain development
   Gerhardt, S. (2014). *Why Love Matters: How Affection Shapes a Baby's Brain*. Routledge.

6. Book describing how to match value hierarchies in relationships
   Demartini, J. F. (2007). *The Heart of Love: How to Go Beyond Fantasy to Find True Relationship Fulfillment*. Hay House.

7. Book describing different types of attachment and the implications of them
   Holmes, J. (2014). *John Bowlby and Attachment Theory*. Routledge.

8. Book describing inner child healing
   Bradshaw, J. (1999). *Home Coming: Reclaiming and Championing Your Inner Child*. Piatkus.

9. Review article on oxytocin-induced brain plasticity
Pekarek, B. T., Hunt, P. J., & Arenkiel, B. R. (2020). Oxytocin and sensory network plasticity. *Frontiers in Neuroscience, 14*, 30. https://doi.org/10.3389/fnins.2020.00030

10. Enhanced memory for stressful experiences
McIntyre, C. K., & Roozendaal, B. (2007). Adrenal Stress Hormones and Enhanced Memory for Emotionally Arousing Experiences. In F. Bermúdez-Rattoni (Ed.), *Neural Plasticity and Memory: From Genes to Brain Imaging*. CRC Press.

11. Article assessing the effectiveness of Gottman's couples therapy approach
Davoodvandi, M., Navabi Nejad, S., & Farzad, V. (2018). Examining the effectiveness of Gottman couple therapy on improving marital adjustment and couples' intimacy. *Iranian Journal of Psychiatry, 13*(2), 135–141.

12. Article on effectiveness of Gottman's couples therapy for homosexual couples
Garanzini, S., Yee, A., Gottman, J., Gottman, J., Cole, C., Preciado, M., & Jasculca, C. (2017). Results of Gottman method couples therapy with gay and lesbian couples. *Journal of Marital and family therapy, 43*(4), 674–684. https://doi.org/10.1111/jmft.12276

Chapter Nine

1. Great book on non-violent communication
Rosenberg, M. B. (2015). *Nonviolent Communication: A Language of Life: Life-Changing Tools for Healthy Relationships*. PuddleDancer Press.

2. An original book describing Gottman's research on relationship dynamics
Gottman, J., & Silver N. (1994). *Why Marriages Succeed or Fail*. Simon & Schuster.

3. Book covering couples therapy that originated from collaboration between John Gottman and his wife, clinical psychologist Julie Gottman

   Gottman, J., Gottman, J., Abrams, R., & Abrams, D. (2019). *Eight Dates: To Keep Your Relationship Happy, Thriving and Lasting.* Penguin Life.

4. Book on Imago conversations in couples

   Hendrix, H., & LaKelly Hunt, H. (2017). *The Space Between.* CloverCroft Publishing.

5. Book on the five languages of love

   Chapman, G. (2015). *The 5 Love Languages: The Secret to Love That Lasts.* MoodyPublishers.

6. A book on using The Work method in relationships

   Katie, B., & Mitchell, S. (2008). *I Need Your Love – Is That True?: How to Find All the Love, Approval and Appreciation you Ever Wanted.* Ebury Digital.

7. Neuroscience research on aggression

   Siegel, A., & Victoroff, J. (2009). Understanding human aggression: New insights from neuroscience. *International Journal of Law and Psychiatry, 32*(4), 209–215. https://doi.org/10.1016/j.ijlp.2009.06.001

8. Polyvagal theory explaining why we react differently to stressors

   Porges, S. W. (2009). The polyvagal theory: New insights into adaptive reactions of the autonomic nervous system. *Cleveland Clinic Journal of Medicine, 76*(4 suppl 2), S86–S90. https://doi.org/10.3949/ccjm.76.s2.17

9. Effects of a happy marriage on the brain

   Radua, J. (2018). Frontal cortical thickness, marriage and life satisfaction. *Neuroscience, 384*, 417–418. https://doi.org/10.1016/j.neuroscience.2018.05.044

10. Research on empathy and compassion
Singer, T., & Klimecki, O. M. (2014). Empathy and compassion. *Current Biology, 24*(18), PR875–R878. https://doi.org/10.1016/j.cub.2014.06.054

11. Article on teaching compassion-based communication skills
Kelley, K. J., & Kelley, M. F. (2013). Teaching empathy and other compassion-based communication skills. *Journal for Nurses in Professional Development, 29*(6), 321–324. https://doi.org/10.1097/01.NND.0000436794.24434.90

ACKNOWLEDGEMENTS

I had a great time creating this content and writing this book. Needless to say, though, that would not have been possible had I not had such great support from my family, collaborators and mentors. First of all, I want to thank my amazing husband Matthew Kevin John Pigden for his unconditional support in my career pursuits and for being amazing dad to our daughter Emilija Luna Pigden. Equally, I am extremely grateful for my mum-in-law, Jane Pigden, for moving in with us and being invaluable help in looking after Emija, and for making our house into a real home. I also want to thank my mum, Ramute Toleikiene, for encouraging my siblings and me to pursue education paths that were most inspiring for us. I would like to also thank my dad, Antanas Toleikis (RIP), for sharing with me his love of books and learning and for showing me the miracle of activity-dependent brain plasticity. In fact, he was one of the main reasons I got interested in neuroscience in the first place as I saw him regain most of his cognitive and mental functions with extensive training after three ischemic strokes.

I am also extremely grateful to my mentors and collaborators Professor Vincent Walsh and Professor Paul Brown, who have helped me advance on my journey in applied neuroscience. I am thankful for Cathy Lasher and Sue Stockdale for providing great training and mentorship in my training as a business coach. I am also thankful for the people who provided me with opportunities to do research in their laboratories over ten years: Professor Osvaldas Ruksenas (Vilnius University, Lithuania), Pertti Panula

(Helsinki University, Finland) and Professor Michael Hausser (University College London, UK). I not only learnt invaluable insights into brain research and state-of-art methodologies there, but was also surrounded by brilliant researchers (in particular Christoph Schmidt-Hieber and Ville Sallinen) whose love and dedication for research and whose supervision were invaluable in my development as a researcher. I also feel grateful for all the researchers whose work I cite in this book for working so hard to make a real difference in the world.

Moreover, I want to thank all of my coaching clients and the attendees of my seminars and workshops, who have provided me with opportunities to develop and tweak the content I am presenting in this book. Last but not least, I want to thank my brilliant agent Kate Barker and the Thread team for making this book come true.